PESTALOZZI

PESTALOZZI

By

Lewis Flint Anderson

AMS PRESS, INC.
NEW YORK

Reprinted from the edition of 1931, New York
First AMS EDITION published 1970
Manufactured in the United States of America

International Standard Book Number: 0-404-00357-5

Library of Congress Catalog Card Number: 75-130984

AMS PRESS, INC.
NEW YORK, N.Y. 10003

TO MY WIFE

PREFACE

IN COMPILING the accompanying selections the aim has been to present in chronological order passages which are characteristic of Pestalozzi's educational writings at successive stages of his career and which will at the same time aid the reader to a fairly accurate conception of his work as a whole.

The general introduction affords a survey of the outstanding features of Pestalozzi's work. The other introductions review the circumstances under which the successive extracts, respectively, were written.

The brief extract from *Leonard and Gertrude* is reprinted from the abridged translation by Eva Channing, published by D. C. Heath & Co. The passage from *Christopher and Alice* is a reprint from Barnard's *American Journal of Education*. The extracts from *How Gertrude Teaches Her Children* are translations by Lucy E. Holland and Frances C. Turner, published by C. W. Bardeen. The *Letters to Greaves* are as published in England in 1827. The remaining selections have been translated by the editor from the Seyffarth edition, *Pestalozzi's sämtliche Werke,* Liegnitz, 1899–1902, and from those volumes of the Buchenau, Spranger, and Stettbacher edition which have so far appeared.

Acknowledgment is due to Professor Edward H. Reisner for having carefully read the manuscript.

LEWIS FLINT ANDERSON

THE OHIO STATE UNIVERSITY

June 1931

CONTENTS

ix

I

INTRODUCTION

ONE will search in vain in the writings of Pestalozzi for any presentation of a complete and unified system of educational theory. Nor can any such system be constructed through an arrangement of selections from his writings. He presents himself to the reader not as a prophet, not as an educational authority, but as a seeker after truth, as a student and investigator of the great problem of the education of man. His writings record, not the discovery of, but the eager, unremitting search for a system of educational procedure that will best contribute to render human beings, and especially the poor, capable of worthy, useful, and hence happy lives.

The purpose of this introduction is to review, in brief compass, certain of the outstanding features of Pestalozzi's work which are exemplified or reflected in the following selections, and which may serve to explain its importance in the history of educational thought and practice.

In the first place, Pestalozzi's approach to the problems of education was unique. It was not that of a professional clergyman and educator, like Comenius, nor was it that of a leader in a revolt against the conditions and tendencies of his time, like Rousseau. It was that of one who, with a definite and immensely important problem to solve, finds in education its only solution.

Owing partly to certain extraordinary innate traits of character, partly to the peculiarities of his early home life, and partly to certain movements and tendencies of his age which found a center in the College of Zürich, which he attended, Pestalozzi early devoted himself to the cause of the elevation of the lives of the poor. The tragic spectacle of the material and mental poverty and wretchedness of a large proportion of his fellow human beings became to him almost an obsession. To the relief of this condition he devoted himself throughout the rest of his life with a steadfastness of purpose and a self-forgetting devotion that finds few parallels in history. As to his central purpose in life Pestalozzi is definite and emphatic.

Ah! long enough! ever since my youth, has my heart moved on like a mighty stream, alone and lonely, towards my one sole end—to stop the sources of the misery in which I saw the people around me sunk. (*How Gertrude Teaches Her Children.*)

In an address to the people during the following year, prefacing his work, *The Natural Schoolmaster,* he writes,

I have seen your misery, your deepest misery, and my heart goes out to you. Dear people I will help you. I have no art, I have no science, and am, in this world, nothing, nothing at all; but I know you and give myself to you. I give you what throughout the long struggle of my life I have been able to accomplish solely for you. (Seyffarth, 9, 365.)

What made of the philanthropist not merely an educator but the founder of an epoch-making school of educational research was his early conviction that the chief source of the misery which he sought to relieve was to be found in the defective nature, the defective abilities of individuals, and that this defect could be remedied through right education. The idea which throughout his life served as the mainspring of his activities was that, for the oppressed poor, the road to fullness of life, and hence to happiness, lay through the promotion, through true education, of the natural development of the mental and physical powers of individuals, hitherto neglected or misdirected.

Here we have one of Pestalozzi's important contributions to the cause of elementary education, the education common to all. He raises it to a higher plane. It ceases to be a mere matter of drill in the three R's and the catechism, to be carried on by tailors and cobblers as a supplementary occupation. It becomes definitely a process of ennobling and enriching human life, one of the most important and beneficent occupations in which man can engage.

But not only did Pestalozzi win recognition for the importance, the loftiness of purpose of elementary education. He inaugurated a movement for raising it from the status of a merely empirical and conventional process to that of one truly scientific.

Possessed of an unusually keen sense of the actualities of life he sought to construct a path toward his goal on a basis of fact. Influenced in part by the naturalistic movement of his time, he recognized that the mind as well as the body which he wished to educate is a natural product, a part of "Nature," and that education, as he conceived it, is a process constantly taking place in nature. At the outset of his career and under the influence of the above movement he was inclined to rely too exclusively upon the educational influences of nonhuman, external nature. Further experience led him to the realization that nature is blind and needs to be directed and supplemented by intelligence, by a conscious "Art" of education.

The inauguration of a movement to adjust deliberate, systematic education to all other influences contributing to the physical, intellectual, and moral development of the individual is one of the important contributions of Pestalozzi to the cause of education.

A characteristic of Pestalozzi as an educational thinker is the clarity of vision with which he traces the educational influences operative in ordinary life. For this he was indebted in part, perhaps, to the fact that he was primarily a philanthropist and not a professional educator. His survey of the life about him was not restricted by the traditions, habits, and conventions which are likely to impose themselves upon those who are engaged in teaching as a vocation. His interest was, primarily, not in schools but in an education which would contribute to the elevation of the lives of the masses. Pestalozzi's keen sense of reality led him to see that education begins at birth and that the institution peculiarly adapted by its very nature to exert incomparably the most powerful influence upon the physical, moral, and intellectual development of the child was the home. For Pestalozzi the home was the one institution of supreme importance as a center of educational influence for the young. Upon its efficiency in promoting the natural development of the child he believed the welfare of mankind to depend. Correlative to this was his conviction that the mother is the person whose natural instincts and whose relationship to the child adapted her above all others to be its educator. The school was given by Pestalozzi a place in his scheme of education only when further experience and study led him to recognize it as an indispensable supplement to the home. It should be noted in this connection that the promotion of cooperation between the school and the home which Pestalozzi recommended has been an outstanding feature of the progressive educational work of the last few years.

Just as Pestalozzi finds through direct inspection of the everyday life about him what the centers are in which the education of the child is to be carried on and who are the natural directors of this process, so he finds here also guidance in the matter of educational procedure. The development of power which he seeks to promote he finds to occur everywhere as a result of the exercise of power. Faculties are strengthened through use. This is adopted as a fundamental principle in Pestalozzian instruction and training.

An examination of the life about him shows him further that the occasion for this exercise is afforded the child normally by the objects immediately about him. This interaction with his immediate surroundings not only conduces to the development of his powers but meets his most immediate need, namely, that of ability to control or to adjust himself to his immediate surroundings. This principle that the child's ordinary surroundings should be used as a means of exercising his powers, is one to which Pestalozzi constantly recurs in his writings. Its observance, particularly as regards the training of the powers of observation, of expression, and of thought, constituted one of the striking features of the educational practice both of himself and of his followers. Ordinarily and naturally the child passes from dealing with his nearest surroundings to those successively more remote.

Here the necessity of intelligent control, of an "Art" of instruction and training presents itself. The child must not be left to chance, to the random influences of blind nature. The adequate development of the child's powers demands that its activities be directed by a mother and assistant educators who, so far as possible, are informed as to what the powers are which are to be trained, in what order, and by what means, they may best be trained. To the investigation of these problems Pestalozzi devoted the greater part of his life. For information he had recourse not to books but to the direct study of the mind, to observation, experiment and reflection. The procedure in promoting the development of the child's mental powers must be adjusted to the nature of the child's mind. Pestalozzi himself characterized his educational efforts as "an attempt to psychologize education." Though not himself a trained scientific investigator, he pointed out to others the way along which solutions to the problem of education are to be approached. With him scientific pedagogy may be said to begin.

Like Rousseau he notes that the course of development of the different mental powers is not parallel and, like him, he combats the besetting evil of the educational practice of the time, that of making premature demands upon the pupil.

Intelligently regulated education, the "Art," should follow nature in providing not merely specialized but all-round, "harmonious" development. An examination of the facts of life, however, shows clearly the direction which man's progress upward is taking. Deliberate, conscious education should follow that of nature in promoting the development of those powers which distinguish man from the lower animals. (cf. p. 219.)

It was, probably, Pestalozzi's clear realization of the fact that "It is life that educates" and his constant reference to the operation of the educational processes in the life about him which led him to see that an understanding of the surrounding world is to be attained by the child not so much through becoming acquainted with the multiplicity of things of which it consists—an end which Comenius and Basedow endeavored to make practicable through their encyclopedias, the *Orbis Pictus* and the *Elementarwerk*—but rather through a cultivation of the powers of observation which would make him capable of distinguishing what was important and essential in any part of the world of reality to which he might be directed.

Whereas Comenius and others recognize the importance of sense perception, direct observation, as a factor in the educative process Pestalozzi aims to cultivate the capacity for *Anschauung,* direct consciousness, experience, not only of the objects of the outer world but of the operations of the mind itself.

In his examination of the mental aspects of the life of his day Pestalozzi seems to have been more or less unconsciously influenced by the opinion, generally current in his time, that the stages of individual development correspond one by one to those of the development of the race, and that the knowledge and skill of the race have developed gradually from the simplest elements of these, respectively. This led him to the conclusion that instruction and training in any field should begin with the elements and should proceed toward the more complex in careful, unbroken gradations.

Much time and effort were devoted by Pestalozzi to the search for the natural, which in his time meant the logical, beginning-points of knowledge, the elements of knowledge and art (HG.,[1] 141). The current practice of beginning with the three R's he believed to be merely conventional and without any basis in nature or reason (HG., 141). An examination of "how a cultivated man behaves—when he wishes to distinguish any object which appears misty and confused before his eyes" afforded him, he believed, the information which he sought. Just as the man, under these circumstances will observe "(1) how many and what kinds of objects are before him; (2) their appearance, form, or outline; (3) their names," so "it must be an immutable law of the Art (1) to teach children to look upon every object— as a unit; (2) to teach them the form of every object; and (3) as soon as possible to make them acquainted with all the words and names descriptive of objects known to them." In other words he concludes that "Number, form and language are together, the elementary means of instruction." This view he finds to be further confirmed by the fact that "The whole sum of the external properties of any object is comprised in its outline and its number, and is brought home to my consciousness through language." (HG., 146.) Still further confirmation he finds in the fact that "All possible objects have absolutely number, form and names; but the other characteristics, known through our five senses, are not common to all objects." (HG., 147.)

[1] This abbreviation will be used for Pestalozzi's *How Gertrude Teaches Her Children.*

8

Such are the considerations which account for the frequency with which the terms "Number, form, and language" occur in the educational writings of Pestalozzi and for the importance attached to these as parts of the elementary curriculum.

The practical experience later acquired by Pestalozzi seems to have shaken his faith somewhat in the validity of this principle. In his last work, *The Swan Song,* the beginning steps in intellectual education are described as (1) careful observation leading to the formation of clear ideas, (2) the expression of these in speech, and (3) reflective thinking.

Observation leads Pestalozzi to the conclusion that moral, like intellectual, education takes its rise in *Anschauung,* in this case in the feeling or experience (*Anschauung*) of love. Like Rousseau, he believes this to arise in the infant in response to loving care of the mother, or others who contribute to its comforts and satisfactions.

If the child enjoys all that parenthood implies, even at the hand of strangers, he receives an impression of love, and he loves in return.

This education, begun in the family circle is continued in the relationships which he forms with those outside. Later this love which originates in the satisfaction of his wants by others comes more and more as his powers mature to find satisfaction in gratifying the needs of others.

As his power grows,—he receives powerful and appropriate stimuli towards affection and activity in love, which gave him so much pleasure in his earlier years. (*Views and Experiences,* Letter 6.)

Pursuing his investigations further Pestalozzi finds that, in life as it is actually lived about him, not only human but nonhuman nature plays a part in fostering the growth of love and sympathy. Nature, as well as parents and friends, contributes what is needed for the satisfaction of the child's wants—"bread as stilling his hunger, water as quenching his thirst, the pear, the grape, the cherry, as pleasing his appetite." (Letter 7.) Moreover he finds in nature pleasant companionship.

The sheep, the cock, the dove, and every living object now gladden the child. His confidence in the life that surrounds him increases, he is happy in this growing confidence, and as he places some beloved and trusted pet upon his mother's lap he is filled with joy.

The appreciation of the beauty of nature tends to make him gentle, kindly, refined.

He cannot look upon the splendor of the setting and rising sun, or that of the moon and stars, without joy. The flowers and the tree laden with fruit delight him.—Inclined (through his early education in the family circle) to be good and gentle, every impression of Nature, the sight of the great works of God, the sky and the earth, tends to make him still more gentle.

II

THE EVENING HOURS OF A HERMIT

THE VARIOUS conditions and circumstances which led Pestalozzi while still a youth to devote himself to the elevation of the lives of the poor are described in the opening pages of his *Views and Experiences* (see pp. 97 to 98, following). It was this aim which, more than any other, seems to have guided him in the selection of a vocation. After some consideration of the Christian ministry and of the practice of law, Pestalozzi decided to take up agriculture. In this selection he was, no doubt, also influenced by a tendency of his time fostered by Rousseau and the naturalistic movement. His farming operations proving unsuccessful, he, following what was becoming more and more a central aim in life, converted his farm establishment at Neuhof into an institution for providing education and work for poor children. This enterprise also proved a failure. Amidst the poverty and disgrace which his failure entailed, he, upon the advice of two faithful friends, Füssli and Iselin, had recourse to his pen. In 1780 *The Evening Hours of a Hermit* appeared in installments in Iselin's periodical, the *Ephemerides*. In a letter to Iselin, Pestalozzi calls this the prologue to everything that he would write hereafter (Seyffarth, 3, 112). The earliest of Pestalozzi's educational writings, it reveals the breadth of his conception of the task to which he came to devote himself with such passionate intensity. In 1807 the aphorisms which constitute the work were rearranged and grouped under headings for publication in an *Educational Weekly* issued by Pestalozzi and his colleagues at Yverdon. The following is a translation of the first half of the work as it appeared originally in 1780.

The Evening Hours of a Hermit, 1780

Man who is one and the same whether on a throne or in a cottage, what in his innermost nature is he? Why do not the wise tell us? Why do not the most highly endowed of the human race learn what man really is? Does the peasant make use of his ox without studying him? Does not the herdsman seek to familiarize himself with the nature of his sheep?

And you who make use of man and say that you protect and nurture him, do you bestow upon him the care that the peasant does upon his ox? Do you trouble yourselves about him as the herdsmen do about their sheep? Does your wisdom consist in a thorough understanding of your race and is your goodness the goodness of enlightened shepherds of the people?

What man is, what his needs are, what elevates and what degrades him, what invigorates and what weakens him, that is what it is necessary for the highest and for the humblest to know.

Men feel the need of this everywhere. Everywhere man is toiling and straining and struggling upward. Because of lack of this knowledge successive generations wither away with their lives unfulfilled and at the end of life the majority of mankind cry aloud that the completion of their course has not satisfied them. Their end is not the ripening of the perfect fruit which having completed the pre-destined course of development sinks to the rest of the winter.

Why does man grope after the truth without system or purpose? Why does he not try to discover the fundamental needs of his nature in order that he may base upon this the enjoyment and the blessedness of his life? Why does he not seek truth, which is peace and the enjoyment of life, truth which satisfies his innermost cravings, which develops his powers, gladdens his days and endows his life with happiness?

Man under the compulsion of his needs finds the road to this truth in his innermost being.

The infant, its hunger satisfied, learns in this way what his mother is to him. She calls forth love, the essence of gratitude, in him before he can utter the words, "duty" or "gratitude." The son who eats his father's bread and warms himself at his hearth finds by this path of nature his happiness in the duties of the child.

Man! if you seek the truth through this means provided by nature you will find it as you need it for your particular case and for your career.

Man! just as it is indispensable to your rest and peace, as it is thy guiding star in thy immediate affairs, just as it is the support on which thy life rests so it is to you an inestimable blessing.

You cannot in this course make use of all truths.

The circle of knowledge by which one in man's situation

may be really benefitted is narrow, and this circle begins immediately around him, around his nearest relationships, extends thence outward and must at every extension regulate itself according to this centre of all the beneficent power of truth.

The pure feeling for truth develops in a limited field. Pure human wisdom rests upon the firm basis of the knowledge of one's immediate relationships and of a capacity for management that has been trained in the handling of one's most intimate affairs.

This human wisdom which reveals itself in the necessities of our situation, strengthens and develops our effectiveness. The type of mind which it calls forth is simple and clear-sighted. Moulded under the powerful influence of contact with things as they are actually related to each other in real life it is easily directed to every side of truth. (It is easily led to deal with every aspect of truth.)

It manifests itself in a feeling of power and in the right application of this.

Sublime path of Nature, the truth to which thou leadest is power and deed, the source of development, the inspiration and the destiny of human nature.

Truly thou formest man not in a hasty, flashy growth, and the son of Nature is restricted, his speech is the expression and the outcome of complete knowledge of the subject. But if men exceed thy pace they work confusion within themselves and dissolve the peace and the equilibrium of their innermost natures.

They do this whenever, instead of rendering their minds obedient to truth and wisdom through first-hand knowledge of actual objects, they plunge into the thousandfold confusion of verbal instruction and opinions and make sound and speech instead of truth and actual objects the foundation of their mental structure and of the earliest cultivation of their powers.

This artificial procedure of the school which everywhere forges ahead of the quiet, orderly, slow procedure of Nature in the matter of speech gives man a superficial polish which conceals the lack of natural power within and gratifies times like ours.

The standpoint of actual life, the actual condition and circumstances of the individual man is the book of nature. In these the power and the method (*Ordnung*) of this wise guide are to be looked for, and every school education, which is not based upon the foundation of the natural education of man, leads astray.

Man! father of thy children, do not compel them to dissipate their powers on remote objects before they have acquired strength through exercising it on their immediate surroundings, and beware of severity and strain.

The power of Nature although it leads irresistibly to truth is not rigid and formal in its action; the song of the nightingale trills through the darkness and all nature rolls on in vitalizing freedom. Nowhere is there a suggestion of a restrictive routine.

Were there a rigid and compulsory procedure in the education of Nature, she also would develop one-sidedness and her truth would not gently and freely nourish the whole nature of man.

The repulsive, exhausting effort to attain the mere shadows of truth; the struggle for the mere tone and sound and verbal images of truth, where no interest attracts and delights and no application is possible; the misdirection of all the powers of the developing human being in the pursuit of the opinion of severe, and one-sided teachers and the thousand and one little arts of word-trafficking and of the latest fashion in teaching which are put forward to serve as a foundation for the education of man; all this is a laborious leading astray from the path of Nature.

In consequence of this harsh procedure truth becomes neither the gentle servant of mankind, nor the kindly sympathetic mother whose happiness and wisdom is the happiness and the need of her children.

Man loses the equilibrium of his strength, the power of his wisdom if his mind is directed too one-sidedly and too powerfully toward one object. This is why the instructional procedure of Nature is never violent.

Nevertheless there is firmness in her training and in her arrangements there is the strict orderliness of the careful housekeeper.

Nor is the confusion resulting from a too eager pursuit of knowledge any nearer the course of Nature.

The man who hovers around and lightly tastes of every branch of knowledge and fails to develop strength through the quiet steady application of knowledge, he also deviates from the path of Nature, he loses that steady, clear, attentive glance, that calm, quiet feeling for truth receptive to real happiness.

Faltering and uncertain will be the course of those men who in the multiplicity of their knowledge find much occasion for talk, but who have sacrificed to it the quiet sense of pure human wisdom. Notwithstanding their noisy pride, their immediate surroundings are to them barren and obscure while those of the truly wise are lighted up by the light of intelligent understanding.

The education of man to truth is the education of his nature to that wisdom which brings calmness and serenity.

Where art thou, power of Nature, thou who dost really train and develop mankind? Even the dead and empty wastes of gloomy ignorance lead one astray from thy path. (As well as the noisy pride above mentioned.)

Want of acquaintanceship with thine own nature, O Man, will place greater restrictions upon thy knowledge than will thy necessities. Distortion of the first fundamental ideas of thy relationship to others; murderous, oppressive power of tyranny; withholding of all enjoyment of truth and blessedness; unnatural lack of a general national understanding of the foremost and most essential needs and relationships of mankind; how thy gloomy shadow darkens the world!

Hence the fully developed power of mankind, this source of their mighty deeds and of their quiet enjoyment is no merely imaginary impulse and no deceptive illusion.

Satisfaction of the innermost needs of our being, pure power of our nature, thou blessing of our existence, thou art no dream! To seek and search for thee is the aim and destiny of mankind and my need and the yearning of my innermost soul is to seek thee, thou aim and destiny of mankind.

Where and how shall I find thee, Truth, who art my salvation and who exaltest me to the perfection of my nature?

In my inner nature is to be found the gateway to this truth. All mankind are fundamentally alike and for the satisfaction of their needs there is one and the same way.

Hence the truth which will be discovered in our innermost being will apply to mankind at large and it will serve as a unifying influence to bring together those who by thousands are quarreling over mere externals.

The pure and beneficent powers of mankind are not the gifts of art or of accident. In our inner nature they lie bound up with our fundamental tendencies and capacities. Their development is the fundamental need of mankind. Therefore the path of nature which reveals it must be open and easy. It must be simple and capable of use by the rank and file of humanity for the education of man to true and tranquillizing wisdom.

Nature develops all the powers of mankind through exercise, and their growth results from use.

The procedure of Nature in the development of mankind is that of application and of making use of its knowledge, of its endowments and talents.

Hence it is the man of simple and upright character, who, since he with pure and humble application of his knowledge and with quiet industry uses and exercises every one of his capacities and talents, is educated by Nature to true human wisdom. On the other hand the man who destroys within himself this orderly process of Nature and weakens the sense of the conformity of his knowledge (to Nature) becomes incapable of the enjoyment of truth.

Actions that do violence to that inner feeling of justice, undermine our capacity for apprehending the truth, they confuse our clear sense of the lofty and noble simplicity of our fundamental ideas and of our fundamental feelings.

Hence all human wisdom rests upon the power of a good

heart obedient to the truth, and all human blessedness upon this sense of simplicity and uprightness.

Education of mankind to this pure sense of simplicity and uprightness, thou art the fatherly care of mankind that the uncorrupted fundamental impulses of the heart protect the course of its mental and spiritual development and rightly guide it.

The general building-up of these inner powers of man's nature to pure human wisdom is the general aim of the education even of the humblest and lowest.

The exercise, application and use of his strength and wisdom in the particular situations and circumstances of mankind is vocational and class education. This must always be subordinate to the general aim of the education of man.

Wisdom and strength based upon simplicity and virtue is a blessing in every variety of circumstance in which human beings live, even in the lowest, just as it is an indispensable necessity at every height in the social scale.

Whoever is not a man, is not a man with his native capacities fully developed, lacks the foundation on which to base his preparation for a definite vocation and for his particular place in life—a defect for which no rank in society, however high may serve as an excuse.

A wide gulf separates the ordinary father of a family and the prince, the poor man burdened with anxiety for his daily bread and the rich groaning with the burden of still heavier cares, the ignorant woman and the famous savant, the idle sluggard and the soaring genius whose influence is felt throughout the world.

Yet if the one in his lofty station is lacking in true humanity dark clouds will gather about him while, in the humble cottages of the poor, cultivated humanity radiates pure, exalted and contented human greatness.

So in his lofty position a prince may seek wise and just laws for offenders against the law yet perhaps he may spend his money in vain. If he wishes to manifest, however, the truly paternal spirit in the council of war, in the hunt, in the management of his lands and of his household he will educate judges and warders of the criminal classes to be wise, earnest and fatherly in spirit.

Otherwise the talk about enlightened laws is like the talk of the love of one's neighbor by those whose hearts are devoid of love.

So far are you, perhaps, O prince, from attaining the blessedness of the truth which you seek.

Meanwhile fathers in the dust beneath thy feet are acting wisely in dealing with foolish sons. Prince, learn in the tears of their night watches and in the toil and trouble of their daily life how to deal wisely with offenders and give thy right over life and death to men who seek wisdom by this path. O Prince, a truly cultivated humanity is a blessing to the world. Only through it does the might of enlightenment and of wisdom manifest itself. It alone makes laws a boon to mankind.

Man! thou thyself, the inner awareness of thy being and of thy powers is the first object of the creative, developing activity of Nature. But you do not live for yourself alone. Hence Nature fits you for external relationships and by means of these.

Just in proportion as these relationships are close at hand

are they important for the moulding of thy character so as to adapt it to thy calling in life.

The power developed through interaction with the immediate environment is always the source of the wisdom and power of man in dealing with the more remote.

A fatherly spirit fits one for the position of ruler, a brotherly spirit for that of the citizen; both give rise to system and order in the home and in the state.

The domestic relationships of mankind are the earliest and the most excellent of the relationships of Nature.

Man labors at his vocation and bears the burden of the state and government in order that he may enjoy his domestic happiness in peace.

Hence the training of the man for his calling and station in life must be subordinated to the aim of fitting him to appropriate the pure happiness of home life.

Hence the home is the place where the natural educational process runs its course.

Home! thou school of morals and of the state!

First thou art a child, a human being, only afterwards an apprentice of thy trade or profession.

The virtues of childhood should bear fruit in the period of apprenticeship and they should afford the earliest training of thy capacity for the enjoyment of all the blessings of thy life.

Whoever turns aside from this order of nature and gives precedence contrary to nature to class, vocational training, training for ruling or serving, leads mankind away from the enjoyment of the most natural blessings to a sea of dangers and difficulties.

Man must be trained to inner peace. Contentment with his lot and with attainable pleasures, patience, carefulness, faith in the love of the Father in the face of every hindrance, that is education to human wisdom.

Without inner peace man wanders on wild pathways. The eager urge to attain impossibly distant goals deprives him of all enjoyment of his immediate surroundings and of all the strength of the wise, patient and obedient nature.

If feeling is not suffused with inner peace its force enervates man in his inner being and afflicts him with sorrow and anguish under circumstances which the wise endure with smiling contentment.

Peace and quiet enjoyment are the first ends of human education and the greatest needs of the time. Man! thy knowledge and ambition must be subordinated to these higher aims. Otherwise envy and ambition will be a source of pain and unhappiness. . . .

III

LEONARD AND GERTRUDE

DURING the year following that of the publication of *The Evening Hours of a Hermit*, Pestalozzi published the first part of *Leonard and Gertrude*, the work which, more than any other, contributed to make his name known throughout Europe. His profound knowledge of the conditions of peasant life, based upon years of direct and sympathetic observation; his passionate absorption in the project of relieving the poor of the hardships, the disabilities which they needlessly endured, and his firm conviction that he had discovered the means of bringing this about, inspired him to paint a picture of the wretchedness of village life so vivid and moving, and a picture of its regeneration so attractive as to arouse widespread interest throughout Europe.

One source of the beneficent influences which contribute to the elevation of the life of the village as a whole is the effective education afforded the children in the well-ordered home of Gertrude, the wife of a village mason. The following is one of various passages descriptive of the everyday life of the home and of its educational influence.

———

23

Leonard and Gertrude

GERTRUDE'S METHOD OF INSTRUCTION

It was quite early in the morning when Arner, Glülphi and the pastor went to the mason's cottage. The room was not in order when they entered, for the family had just finished breakfast, and the dirty plates and spoons still lay upon the table. Gertrude was at first somewhat disconcerted, but the visitors reassured her, saying kindly: "This is as it should be; it is impossible to clear the table before breakfast is eaten!"

The children all helped wash the dishes, and then seated themselves in their customary places before their work. The gentlemen begged Gertrude to let everything go on as usual, and after the first half hour, during which she was a little embarrassed, all proceeded as if no stranger were present. First the children sang their morning hymns, and then Gertrude read a chapter of the Bible aloud, which they repeated after her while they were spinning, rehearsing the most instructive passages until they knew them by heart. In the mean time, the oldest girl had been making the children's beds in the adjoining room, and the visitors noticed through the open door that she silently repeated what the others were reciting. When this task was completed, she went into the garden and returned with vegetables for dinner, which she cleaned while repeating Bible-verses with the rest.

It was something new for the children to see three gentlemen in the room, and they often looked up from their spinning toward the corner where the strangers sat. Gertrude noticed this, and said to them: "Seems to me you look more at these gentlemen than at your yarn." But Harry answered:

24

"No, indeed! We are working hard, and you'll have finer yarn to-day than usual."

Whenever Gertrude saw that anything was amiss with the wheels or cotton, she rose from her work, and put it in order. The smallest children, who were not old enough to spin, picked over the cotton for carding, with a skill which excited the admiration of the visitors.

Although Gertrude thus exerted herself to develop very early the manual dexterity of her children, she was in no haste for them to learn to read and write. But she took pains to teach them early how to speak; for, as she said, "of what use is it for a person to be able to read and write, if he cannot speak?—since reading and writing are only an artificial sort of speech." To this end she used to make the children pronounce syllables after her in regular succession, taking them from an old A-B-C book she had. This exercise in correct and distinct articulation was, however, only a subordinate object in her whole scheme of education, which embraced a true comprehension of life itself. Yet she never adopted the tone of instructor toward her children; she did not say to them: "Child, this is your head, your nose, your hand, your finger"; or: "Where is your eye, your ear?"—but instead, she would say: "Come here, child, I will wash your little hands," "I will comb your hair," or: "I will cut your finger-nails." Her verbal instruction seemed to vanish in the spirit of her real activity, in which it always had its source. The result of her system was that each child was skilful, intelligent and active to the full extent that its age and development allowed.

The instruction she gave them in the rudiments of arithmetic was intimately connected with the realities of life. She taught them to count the number of steps from one end of the room to the other, and two of the rows of five panes each, in one of the windows, gave her an opportunity to unfold the decimal relations of numbers. She also made them count their threads while spinning, and the number of turns on the reel, when they wound the yarn into skeins. Above all, in every occupation of life she taught them an accurate and intelligent observation of common objects and the forces of nature.

All that Gertrude's children knew, they knew so thoroughly that they were able to teach it to the younger ones; and this they often begged permission to do. On this day, while the visitors were present, Jonas sat with each arm around the neck of a smaller child, and made the little ones pronounce the syllables of the A-B-C book after him; while Lizzie placed herself with her wheel between two of the others, and while all three spun, taught them the words of a hymn with the utmost patience.

When the guests took their departure, they told Gertrude they would come again on the morrow. "Why?" she returned, "You will only see the same thing over again." But Glülphi said: "That is the best praise you could possibly give yourself." Gertrude blushed at this compliment and stood confused when the gentlemen kindly pressed her hand in taking leave.

The three could not sufficiently admire what they had seen at the mason's house, and Glülphi was so overcome by the powerful impression made upon him, that he longed to be alone and seek counsel of his own thoughts. He hastened to his room, and as he crossed the threshold, the words broke from his lips: "*I* must be schoolmaster in Bonnal!"

All night visions of Gertrude's schoolroom floated through his mind, and he only fell asleep toward morning. Before his eyes were fairly open, he murmured: "I will be school-master!"—and hastened to Arner to acquaint him with his resolution.

IV

CHRISTOPHER AND ALICE

NOTWITHSTANDING the fame which the publication of *Leonard and Gertrude* brought to Pestalozzi, the results were to him a keen disappointment. Written primarily with the purpose of arousing public interest in a definite plan for enhancing the value of life for the masses, it achieved popularity mainly as a realistic and interesting work of fiction descriptive of life in a peasant village.

In the preface to the second edition, Pestalozzi attempted to direct attention to the real significance of the book. As an additional means of leading the public to use the book for the purpose for which it was intended, he wrote in 1782 a work entitled *Christopher and Alice* depicting the members of a farmer's household as reading the earlier work and discussing the educational ideas which it contains.

Christopher and Alice

HOME AND SCHOOL TRAINING. DOMESTIC EDUCATION

"That is my chapter, father!" said Alice, when Christopher had read the twelfth chapter of our book;[1] "a pious mother,

[1] This chapter represents Gertrude in the midst of her children, teaching them, at the same time that they are engaged in spinning.

who herself teaches her children seems to me to be the finest sight on the earth."

"It is a very different one from a school room, at all events," said Josiah.

Alice. "I did not mean to say that schools are not very good."

Christopher. "Nor would I allow myself to think so."

Josiah. "Well, and it is true, after all, that nothing of what the schoolmaster can say will ever reach children's hearts in the same way as what their parents teach them; and, generally speaking, I am sure there is not in school-going all the good that people fancy there is."

Christopher. "I am afraid, Josiah, thou art rather straining thy point. We ought to thank God for all the good that there is in the world; and, as for the schools in our country, we can't thank Him enough for them."

Josiah. "Well spoken, master. It is well that there are schools; and God forbid that I should be ungrateful for any good that it has done to us. But, with all this, I think that he must be a fool who, having plenty at home, runs about begging; and that is the very thing which our village folks do, by forgetting all the good lessons which they might teach their children at home, and, instead thereof, sending them every day to gather up the dry crumbs which are to be got in our miserable schools. I am sure that is not quite as it ought to be."

Christopher. "Nor is it, perhaps, quite as thou hast put it."

Josiah. "Nay, master! but only look it in the face, and thou'lt surely see it the same as I do. That which parents can teach their children is always what they stand most in need of in life; and it is a pity that parents should neglect this, by trusting in the words which the schoolmaster makes them get by heart. It is very true, they may be good and wise words, and have an excellent meaning to them; but, after all, they are only words, and coming from the mouth of a stranger, they don't come half as near home as a father's or a mother's words."

Christopher. "I can not see what thou would'st be at, Josiah."

Josiah. "Look, master! The great point in bringing up a child is, that he should be well brought up for his own house; he must learn to know, and handle, and use those things on which his bread and his quiet will depend through life; and it seems to me very plain, that fathers and mothers can teach that much better at home, than any schoolmaster can do it in his school. The schoolmaster, no doubt, tells the children of a great many things which are right and good, but they are never worth as much in his mouth as in the mouth of an upright father, or a pious mother. The schoolmaster, for instance, will tell the child to fear God, and to honor his father and mother, for that such is the word of God; but the child understands little of what he says, and mostly forgets it again before he comes home. But if, at home, his father gives him milk and bread, and his mother denies herself a morsel, that she may give it to him, the child feels and understands that he ought to honor his father and mother, who are so kind to him, and he will not forget his father's words, which tell him that such is the word of God, as easily as the empty word of the school-master. In the same way, if the child is told at school to be merciful, and to love his neighbor as himself, he gets the

30

text by heart, and perhaps thinks of it for a few days, till the nice words slip again from his memory. But at home he sees a poor neighbor's wife calling in upon his mother, lamenting over her misery, her hunger, and nakedness; he sees her pale countenance, her emaciated and trembling figure, the very image of wretchedness; his heart throbs, his tears flow; he lifts up his eyes full of grief and anxiety to his mother, as if he himself was starving; his mother goes to fetch some refreshments for the poor sufferer, in whose looks the child now reads comfort and reviving hope; his anguish ceases, his tears flow no longer, he approaches her with a smiling face; at last his mother returns, and her gift is received with sobs of gratitude, which draw fresh tears from the child's eye. Here then he learns what it is to be merciful, and to love one's neighbor. He learns it, without the aid of words, by the real fact; he sees mercy itself, instead of learning words about mercy."

Christopher. "I must own I begin to think thou art not quite mistaken in saying that too much value is put upon the schoolmaster's teaching."

Josiah. "Of course, master! If thou sendest thy sheep up into the mountain, thou reliest upon their being well kept by the shepherd, who is paid for it, and thou dost not think of running about after them thyself; but if thou hast them at home, in thy own stables, thou lookest after them thyself. Now it is just the same thing with the school; only there is this difference, that it is easy to get for the sheep pasture which is infinitely better than the food they have in the stable; but it is not so easy to find a school in which the children are better taught than they might be at home.

The parents' teaching is the kernel of wisdom, and the schoolmaster's business is only to make a husk over it, and there even is a great chance whether it turn out well."

Alice. "Why, Josiah, thou makest one's brains whirl all round, about one's children. I think I see now what thou art at; and I fancy many a poor, ignorant mother, who now sends her children to school, without thinking any thing about it, merely because it is the custom to do so, would be very glad to be taught better."

Josiah. "There is yet another part of the story, master. What helps the common people to get through the world, thou knowest, and to have their daily bread, and a cheerful heart, is nothing else but good sense and natural understanding; and I have never found in all my life a useful man who was what they call a good scholar. The right understanding with the common people is, as it were, free and easy, and shows itself always in the proper place and season; so that a man's words don't fit but at the very moment when they are spoken, and a quarter of an hour before or after they would not fit at all. But the school understanding, brings in all manner of sayings which are fit at all times, in summer and winter, in hot and cold, in Lent and at Easter; and that is the reason why this school understanding does not do any good to common people, who must regulate themselves according to times and seasons; and that is the reason, again, why their natural understandings, which are in them, ought to be drawn out more. And for this, there are no better teachers than the house, and the father's and mother's love, and the daily labor at home, and all the wants and necessities of life. But if the children must needs be sent to school, the schoolmaster should, at least, be an open-hearted, cheerful, affectionate, and kind man, who would be a father to the children; a man made on purpose to open children's hearts, and their mouths, and to draw forth their understandings, as it were, from the hindermost corner. In most schools, however, it is just the contrary; the schoolmaster seems as if he was made on purpose to shut up children's mouths and hearts, and to bury their good understandings ever so deep under ground. That is the reason why healthy and cheerful children, whose hearts are full of joy and gladness, hardly ever like school. Those that show best at school are the children of whining hypocrites, or of conceited parish-officers; stupid dunces, who have no pleasure with other children; these are the bright ornaments of school rooms, who hold up their heads among the other children, like the wooden king in the ninepins among his eight fellows. But, if there is a boy who has too much good sense to keep his eyes, for hours together, fixed upon a dozen letters which he hates; or a merry girl, who, while the schoolmaster discourses of spiritual life, plays with her little hands all manner of temporal fun, under the desk; the schoolmaster, in his wisdom, settles that these are the goats who care not for their everlasting salvation. . . ."

Thus spoke good Josiah, in the overflowing of his zeal, against the nonsense of village schools, and his master and mistress grew more and more attentive to what he said.

"Well, I trust," said Christopher, at last, "there still may be some other light to view the matter in."

But Alice replied: "There may be twenty more lights to view the matter in, for aught I know. But I care not; I know this one thing, that I will have my children more about me in future; it seems very natural, indeed, that fathers and mothers should themselves teach their children as much as they possibly can. I think there is a great deal in what Josiah says, and one really shudders, when one comes to reflect what sort of people our village schoolmasters generally are. There are many of them, I know, Christopher, whom thou wouldst not trust with a cow, or a calf, over winter; and it is very true, that one ought to look more one's self after one's children, and not fancy all is well, provided one sends them to school."

V

THE SWISS NEWS

UNABLE, after the failure of his institution at Neuhof
for the education of waifs and orphans, to engage directly in experiments in the education of the poor,
Pestalozzi conceived the idea of contributing to the
cause of popular enlightenment through the publication of a weekly journal of instruction and entertain-
ment. The plan was realized in the publication
throughout the year 1782 of fifty-two numbers of
The Swiss News (*Ein Schweizer-Blatt*). Among the
numerous articles contributed by Pestalozzi are a number on education. From these the following selections
are taken.

The importance of the home as the natural center
of educational influence, of the immediate, ordinary
surroundings of the child as material on which to exercise his growing powers, hostility toward the modern
"artificial" education of his time are outstanding features of his educational views even at this early stage
of their development. His views as to the adequacy
of industrial handwork as a means of general education were later to undergo modification.

PESTALOZZI

Ein Schweizer-Blatt XXVIII, No. 2

(Seyffarth, Vol. 6. Buchenau, Spranger, and Stettbacher
edition, Vol. 8, p. 284, No. 39)

The first needs of man are bodily and sensory and the
satisfaction of these sensory and bodily needs is what makes
the first educational impression on the child. In other words,
it is the earliest foundation of his education. The earliest
development of his powers and talents depends upon this.
More dependent and helpless than any other creature on
earth, the child experiences at the breast of his mother and
on the lap of his nurse the earliest moral impressions, a
vague feeling of love and gratitude which in poor humanity
is best preserved by a realization of weakness and of con-
tinuing need.

These sensory and bodily needs lead the child gradually
to an all-round development of the capacities of his mind
and his body. Hungry he stretches out his hand for bread
and he walks to the place where his milk is kept. He learns
to win the love of those from whom he desires help, he
seeks to ascertain from your eye what your heart feels for
or against him. He knows the tones of your love, of your
joy or anger because he needs you and on account of his
needs he must give heed to you. So his bodily needs are the
foundation of the development of his powers; they lead
him simply and directly to the double foundation of all true
human wisdom and virtue, namely to gratitude and to love,
which are the foundation of human morality, and to the
struggle for bread, that is, to work, which ensures the morality and virtue of men on earth.

Thus nature develops the capacities of mankind through

the attention of the child to the satisfaction of his bodily wants, and the food-attention of man in his later years is nothing else than the direct continuance along this simple road in which nature so excellently develops and trains every man for his position and circumstances. Hence the advance in man's morality is nothing else than the extension, the more immediate development, the encouragement and modification of the feelings of gratitude and love which the satisfied, refreshed and caressed nursling already feels. Therefore my whole meaning as to the purpose of the education of man amounts simply to this, that one should lead the young along this simple road and endeavor through work and gratitude to develop the morals, the habits and the kinds of skill which each needs in his station.

But then indeed the individual circumstances of man are so infinitely various that it seems to me that if all the animals on earth had to be educated each to his career they would not have to be fitted for more dissimilar situations than has man alone. But if the animals of earth had needed education as our race does they would not send the wolf and the lamb, the fox and the hare to the same school; we would not lay the worms, which crawl upon the earth, upon the back of the eagle in order that they might fly with him toward the sun; we would not place the tiger's food before the elephant and elephant fodder before the tiger; we would not try to nourish the sparrow with ants' eggs and the nightingale with the grain of the fields which is the sparrow's food. But the education of man is very often just such a hodge-podge of sparrows'-food and ants' eggs, of pure elephant fodder and of carrion, which only beasts of prey eat.

Hence it would be a good thing for man, even though he

is lord of the earth, if he should give careful heed to how
the cattle bring up their young; it would be good for him
if he saw and noticed, that the mother of the calf does not
teach the young beast to fly, that the old ass trains his son
in patience and contentment and warns him against the
leaps of the light-footed roebuck and against the dreams of
the fiery steed and against the fondness for oats with which
the more aristocratic beasts of the stall are nourished. It
would be a good thing for man if he saw and noticed that
all the beasts of the earth bring up their young for their
food and if he learned to do this also, and bring up his children for their food. Of course man has powers which raise
him above the beasts of the field who seek only food, but
nevertheless the happiness of his life depends also upon his
finding food and he is not, like the beast, prepared for this
beforehand. Error and vice rob him of his bread and the
child of earth who has been badly brought up cannot use
his talents and powers for his satisfaction, as can the beast
of the field who applies his powers and capacities instinctively
to the certain satisfaction of his wants.

Hence the entire success of human education rests upon
this, that every child should learn to satisfy especially his
sensory and bodily needs. Let it not lead you astray, you
vain and always impatient man, that thy first care for thy
children shall for a long time aim at the satisfaction of
merely their senses and their bodily needs. Care for their
bodies especially as long as their bodily needs demand especial attention. Nature has encased the higher talents of man
as if in a shell; if you break this shell before it opens of
itself you expose an immature pearl and destroy the treasure
of life which you should have preserved for thy child.

Wisdom and virtue is [sic] the late goal of maturing age and the duties of religion are not food for the nursling and its sacrifices are not the play of children.

The premature development of the head and the heart destroys man's real powers and makes of your children what you are yourself if you, impelled by untimely desires, pluck and eat the fruit of your best tree. The development of the head and of the heart up to a point and in a direction which at the end not only fails to satisfy but, on the contrary, causes trouble and unrest, is of no value. If the children about me cry for bread and grow up at my side to be idlers while I solve algebraic problems or estimate the needs of the nation which without my aid might be satisfied, or dream of matters pertaining to eternity, I neglect the first duty which man owes to his creator, the citizen to his fatherland and the father to his child, for this is, plainly, that he should be a good householder and that wife and child should in his house be well cared for.

But indeed it is also true that most men of our time are not to blame if they are not this, for efficient house fathers and house mothers will be generally only those who in their youth were educated for their particular station in life and for making a living. Hence fixed attention to the particular situation of every child is one of the first and most essential of the rules of education, moreover, all more general educational principles which have in mind not a particular, definite individual but the entire human race, easily lead one astray.

Man is in general very incapable of comprehending great, general points of view, and, on the other hand, very apt in rightly comprehending a single definite object and in working himself into a thorough knowledge of it, and one can more easily find a thousand men who are in a position to abstract principles of education from the observation of their own children than a single one who through reflection on nature and the general needs of man makes himself capable in a particular case of educating a particular child for the demands of his particular situation. You are so and so, and you must become this and that, and such and such, said the forefathers, and had clearly in mind what they wished, what they could do, and what must be, and their children fell commonly into this narrow groove.

Man can become a thousand different things and the child must be prepared for everything, we young people say, and we dream visions of mankind, whom we do not know, and pay no attention to the boy whom you call Hans and the boy grows up of no use because we, shrouded in dreams of mankind, forget Hans in whom the man whom we wish to educate grows up.

The principles regulating real human education must not only be true in themselves but also in view of the persons from whom one expects the carrying out of these. Thus considered, the principle, of basing the earliest development of the human powers upon domestic industry is strikingly true, since fathers and mothers who in general are, and should be, the educators of mankind, are always led by a thousand circumstances in their house management to this principle and are educated to it.

To live, to be happy in one's station in life, to be useful in one's sphere is the destiny of man and the goal of the education of children.

Hence the painstaking use of the ways and means by which

every child may be brought easily and naturally to the skill, the disposition, the judgments and attachments through which it may become happy in its station in life and a useful member of society is the foundation of every good education. From this it follows that the means to be employed in educating men to that disposition and skill which will make them happy are just as varied as are their circumstances, their needs and relationships. Hence the general rules of education which are suited to every climate, to all forms of government and to all occupations are no more important than those Sunday sermons which so often edify whole communities and yet so seldom aid a single individual man to the right path.

Meanwhile we should congratulate ourselves that, while the teachers of men from their lofty stations are so indefinite in their accounts of what is right, so often women in country cottages with all definiteness actually carry out what the former merely prate about in empty generalities. And it is an especially fortunate thing for education that the home circumstances of the common people (and that means of the majority) are such that almost everywhere the parents, as if of necessity, naturally and by themselves light upon that which in their circumstances is of most importance for the right education of their children. Were that not the case and did men have to depend upon food from the wise for the nourishment of their children, the race of men would surely die out in all the four corners of the earth. Hence we shall not deny to the unlearned and the obscure of our land the gratitude which we owe them: for truly wherever we look about us it is the ordinary common man who is better educated than the man of the upper classes. For the latter has fallen into the hands of the philosophers, who, in consequence of their studying and abstracting, become daily more and more oblivious of the fact that they possess sight and hearing and hence cannot understand how work in or about the house could have an educational influence upon them or their pupils.

Consider no one happy, said the ancients, until he is dead, and I say, in like manner; praise the wisdom and virtue of no man until you see how he cares for his children and how these respond to his care. Zeal to fulfil the duties of a father is the essence of human virtue, and prudence in the use of the most suitable means to this end is the test stone of genuine human wisdom in its most important field of activity.

And now, men, that you know that experience is the seal of truth, let it be the guiding star which you follow in this most important business; therefore look about you, investigate and seek out among men those who keep their households and their business best in order for they it is who have been best educated for their place in life. Seek out the seats of the nobility, the homes of the citizens and the cottages of the peasants whose standards of living have been maintained for centuries for there the principles of true education have been practiced for centuries.

And, if you find what I have found, you will see that the house management of all these people is everywhere alike; you will find it very simple and you will everywhere see that husband and wife have derived from father and grandfather wisdom and manners the observance of which, will secure the welfare of their house management in the centuries to come as it has in the centuries past.

You will find that it was not the schooling and the systematic instruction which these people had outside the home which moulded the talents, habits, moods and skill by which the prosperity of these houses was founded and by which it is now maintained.

On the other hand you will find domestic ruin and unhappiness among the aristocracy, the middle class and the peasants in just that proportion to which they have deviated from the customs, the tone and manner of life of their ancestors; you will find the cause of the decline of domestic well-being most frequently by far among children whose disposition and culture have not been adapted to their situation, among children who have received an artificial training by strangers who have not recognized the essential educational advantages of their home environment and who have educated them for things out of harmony with what they should be in their home and for their home. You will find the same thing among children whose passions and desires have been adjusted by their thoughtless fathers to a higher standard than they in their limited circumstances can easily satisfy.

You will find that the original causes of the most irreparable domestic ruin often originate in universities, and that they are often fostered in good, but too liberal, educational institutions. Everywhere where the management of men is most highly elaborated and refined you will see these causes appear in the most dangerous form. You will find domestic shipwreck most common among the learned, the clergy, the lawyers, in short among all men in whose education the artificial predominates. You will certainly find that realistic education for the needs of everyday life is everywhere neglected just in proportion as the children are, either through neglect or compulsion, drawn away from attachment to the class and the profession of their family and are lead astray into occupations which promise to be more remunerative than their father's.

Should you doubt the truth of this statement, dear reader, or should it cause you too much trouble to investigate it, go and examine the registers of our civic almshouses and orphan asylums and enquire what kind of citizens and what children are received there. If you do this you will quickly learn the truth of this matter, namely, that neglect of ordinary home education and the withdrawal of the children from the educational influence of their home life and of their father's business is one of the primary causes of the ever-increasing domestic unhappiness. And you will find that methods of education that lead the ordinary citizen away from what is most toilsome and restrictive in his father's occupation and circumstances and prepares his children for something else than for what is most promising and nearest at hand and inoculates them with a desire for the career of a soldier, a professor, a priest, an administrator, financier or barber rather than with a desire to care for their own paternal acres where in old age they may find a secure refuge, you will find, I say, that all these educational methods are faulty and are, therefore, in my eyes one of the great dangers of our times.

Such is the ever-increasing brilliance of the many kinds of education experts whose masterpieces seem so striking and generally beautiful that no one would any longer doubt their perfection did not this brilliant education produce men and women wretchedly deficient in the performance of their domestic duties and obligations, whose proceedings make even the most patient of the slaves of fashion attentive to the general inefficiency of this highly artificial system of education.

If the man is to become what he ought to be, he must as a child be, and as a child do, what will make him happy as a child. He must be, as a child, all, but not more than he can be without injuring himself in that which, in his condition and station in life, he can become as a man. That is, in my opinion, the first fundamental principle of a good education, and it must, in all cases, and in the fullest sense of the term, be the first great goal of the educator and of the father if he has in mind to fit his child for a peaceful domestic life.

It is from this point of view, dear people of the new world, that I, in spite of all the torches of wisdom of our time, honor the simple course of the education of our forefathers; ah they were so direct in their action and so upright, they took delight in the blessed sun at bright noon day. We, however, sleep through the bright day and wander with our children in the gloomy shades of night and, follow the Will-o'-the-wisps, of the blinding mists and lights whose radiance is death for everyone whom they lead astray.

The great secret of the education of our forefathers, by which they avoided so naturally the dangers of the newer artificialities, consisted in this, that they, in all circumstances, and always as soon as possible, sought to derive assistance from their children in their house work. This aim directed them with infinitely greater ease to the fundamental principles of true education than do our new theories, which always tend to draw away attention from the fact that the object is the main thing.

And if I turn to the venerable survivors of the better education period of our forefathers and fix my eye on those men who prove by their lives, by their orderly households, and by notably wise conduct in their station in life, and in their vocation, that they have been well educated, I find them almost everywhere to be people who cordially agree with what I have just said, and if I carefully search into the essential features of their most excellent education for domestic well-being, I never find it to be in the direction they received during their academic years, never in their systems of scientific doctrine, but always in their home conditions, in the circumstances, dispositions and morals of their parents and relatives and a thousand times in things to which, as extremely insignificant trifles, our present age pays almost no attention.

Here a wise father says to me: "For my good fortune and that of my house I have to thank a servant of my father's whose strictness required me to tackle a thousand and one things in and about my home which I should otherwise have ignored, and by which, I now see clearly, I have been made and what I now am." Another says: "My father brought me up as if I would have to earn myself everything which I now possess, and the course of my life has proven to me that if he had not exercised this foresight everything which he left me would have been lost." Still another says: "I have been so thoroughly trained in my trade and occupation that it would seem as if my head and my heart and my five senses had no other destiny on God's earth than that I should live and die in my father's workshop; and now I recognize that for all that I have become in the world and outside the workshop I have to thank the circumstance that I had to pass my youth so strictly and continuously in it." Such is the character of almost all the contributing factors which the wisest men, the fathers of happiest households have mentioned to me as the sources of their prosperity and, in consequence, as the foundations on which an education leading to like results must be based.

VI

HOW GERTRUDE TEACHES HER CHILDREN

FOR NEARLY twenty years, subsequent to the failure of his institution at Neuhof for the education of the poor, Pestalozzi lived in comparative seclusion devoting himself to literary work in the interest of social, political, and educational reform. At last in 1798 after long years of waiting he secured an opportunity of engaging directly in the task to the achievement of which he had devoted his life, namely, the elevation of the lives of the poor through a system of education founded on that of nature and to be worked out in strict accordance with scientific principles. In that year he was appointed by the recently established unitary and republican government to take charge of an institution at Stanz for waifs and orphans. Here he found himself in a position to test out the practicability of the great enterprise over which he had for so many years been brooding, the elevation of the condition of the mass of mankind through the promotion of the development of their capacities. To his delight he found that the improvement of the people through the right sort of education was possible. Eagerly pursuing his experiments at Burgdorf after the closing of the institution at Stanz, he felt by 1800 that sufficient progress had been made in the formulation and testing of principles of educational procedure to justify their publication. By this time the success he had achieved attracted wide attention and many copies of his book were sold. The title, *How Gertrude Teaches Her Children,* served to remind the reader that it presented simply a continuation and elaboration of the ideas presented in *Leonard and Gertrude* for the improvement of the lives of the masses through the prosecution by the mother in the home and by the teacher in the school of a system of educational procedure based upon the nature of the child.

This account of Pestalozzian principles at the stage of development reached by 1800 is presented in the form of a series of fifteen letters addressed by Pestalozzi to his friend Gessner.

How Gertrude Teaches Her Children

EDUCATION ACCORDING TO NATURE

All instruction of man is then only the Art [1] of helping Nature to develop in her own way; and this Art rests essentially on the relation and harmony between the impressions received by the child and the exact degree of his developed powers. It is also necessary in the impressions that are brought to the child by instruction that there should be a sequence, so that beginning and progress should keep pace with the beginning and progress of the powers to be developed in the child. I soon saw that an inquiry into this sequence throughout the whole range of human knowledge,

[1] "The Art," frequently referred to hereafter, is distinguished by a capital A from art generally; it is our "Science and Art of Education," which is here first put on a psychological and scientific basis.

particularly those fundamental points from which the development of the human mind originates, must be the simple and only way ever to attain and to keep satisfactory school and instruction books, of every grade, suitable for our nature and our wants. I saw just as soon that in making these books the constituents of instruction must be separated according to the degree of the growing power of the child; and that in all matters of instruction, it is necessary to determine with the greatest accuracy which of these constituents is fit for each age of the child, in order on the one hand not to hold him back if he is ready; and on the other, not to load him and confuse him with anything for which he is not quite ready.

This was clear to me. The child must be brought to a high degree of knowledge both of things seen and of words before it is reasonable to teach him to spell or read. I was quite convinced that at their earliest age children need psychological training in gaining intelligent sense-impressions of all things. But since such training, without the help of art, is not to be thought of or expected of men as they are, the need of picture-books struck me perforce. These should precede the A-B-C books, in order to make those ideas that men express by words clear to the children (by means of well-chosen real objects, that either in reality, or in the form of well-made models and drawings, can be brought before their minds).

A happy experiment confirmed my then unripe opinion in a striking way (in spite of all the limitations of my means, and the error and one-sidedness in my experiments). An anxious mother entrusted her hardly three-year-old child to my private teaching. I saw him for a time every day for an hour; and for a time felt the pulse of a method with him. I tried to teach him by letters, figures, and anything handy; that is, I aimed at giving him clear ideas and expressions by these means. I made him name correctly what he knew of anything—color, limbs, place, form, and number. I was obliged to put aside that first plague of youth, the miserable letters; he would have nothing but pictures and things.

He soon expressed himself clearly about the objects that lay within the limits of his knowledge. He found common illustrations in the street, the garden, and the room; and soon learned to pronounce the hardest names of plants and animals, and to compare objects quite unknown to him with those known, and to produce a clear sense-impression of them in himself. Although this experiment led to byeways, and worked for the strange and distant to the disadvantage of the present, it threw a many-sided light on the means of quickening the child to his surroundings, and showing him the charm of self-activity in the extension of his powers.

But yet the experiment was not satisfactory for that which I was particularly seeking, because the boy had already three unused years behind him. I am convinced that nature brings the children even at this age to a definite consciousness of innumerable objects. It only needs that we should with psychological art unite speech with this knowledge in order to bring it to a high degree of clearness; and so enable us to connect the foundations of many-sided arts and truths with that which nature herself teaches, and also to use what nature teaches as a means of explaining all the fundamentals of art and truth that can be connected with them. Their power and their experience both are great at this age; but our unpsychological schools are essentially only artificial stifling-machines for destroying all the results of the power and experience that nature herself brings to life in them.

You know it, my friend. But for a moment picture to yourself the horror of this murder. We leave children up to their fifth year in the full enjoyment of nature; we let every impression of nature work upon them; they feel their power; they already know full well the joy of unrestrained liberty and all its charms. The free natural bent which the sensuous happy wild thing takes in his development, has in them already taken its most decided direction. And after they have enjoyed this happiness of sensuous life for five whole years, we make all nature round them vanish from before their eyes; tyrannically stop the delightful course of their unrestrained freedom; pen them up like sheep, whole flocks huddled together, in stinking rooms; pitilessly chain them for hours, days, weeks, months, years, to the contemplation of unattractive and monotonous letters, and (contrasted with their former condition) to a maddening course of life.

I cease describing; else I shall come to the picture of the greater number of schoolmasters, thousands of whom in our days merely on account of their unfitness for any means of finding a respectable livelihood have subjected themselves to the toilsomeness of this position, which they in accordance with their unfitness for anything better look upon as a way that leads little further than to keep them from starvation. How infinitely must the children suffer under these circumstances, or, at least, be spoiled!

THE SEARCH FOR THE LAWS OF HUMAN DEVELOPMENT

The mechanism of physical (human) Nature is essentially subject to the same laws as those by which physical Nature generally unfolds her powers. According to these laws, all instruction should engraft the most essential parts of its subject of knowledge firmly into the very being of the human mind; then join on the less essential gradually but uninterruptedly to the most essential, and maintain all the parts of the subject, even to the outermost, in one living proportionate whole.

I now sought for laws to which the development of the human mind must, by its very nature, be subject. I knew they must be the same as those of physical Nature, and trusted to find in them a safe clue to a universal psychological method of instruction. "Man," said I to myself, while dreamily seeking this clue, "as you recognize in every physical ripening of the complete fruit the result of perfection in all its parts, so consider no human judgment ripe that does not appear to you to be the result of a complete sense-impression of all the parts of the object to be judged; but on the contrary, look upon every judgment that seems ripe before a complete observation (*Anschauung*) has been made as nothing but a worm-eaten and therefore apparently ripe fruit, fallen untimely from the tree."

1. Learn therefore to classify observations and complete the simple before proceeding to the complex. Try to make in every art graduated steps of knowledge, in which every new idea is only a small, almost imperceptible addition to that which has been known before, deeply impressed and not to be forgotten.

2. Again, bring all things essentially related to each other to that connection in your mind which they have in Nature. Subordinate all unessential things to the essential in your idea. Especially subordinate the impression given by the Art to that given by Nature and reality; and give to nothing a greater

weight in your idea than it has in relation to your race in Nature.

3. Strengthen and make clear the impressions of important objects by bringing them nearer to you by the Art, and letting them affect you through different senses. Learn for this purpose the first law of physical mechanism, which makes the relative power of all influences of physical Nature depend on the physical nearness or distance of the object in contact with the senses. Never forget that this physical nearness or distance has an immense effect in determining your positive opinions, conduct, duties, and even virtue.

4. Regard all the effects of natural law as absolutely necessary, and recognize in this necessity the result of her power by which Nature unites together the apparently heterogeneous elements of her materials for the achievement of her end. Let the Art with which you work through instruction upon your race, and the results you aim at, be founded upon natural law, so that all your actions may be means to this principal end, although apparently heterogeneous.

5. But the richness of its charm, and the variety of its free play cause physical necessity, or natural law, to bear the impress of freedom and independence.

Let the results of your art and your instruction, while you try to found them upon natural law, by the richness of their charm and the variety of their free play bear the impression of freedom and independence.

All these laws to which the development of human nature is subject converge towards one centre. They converge towards the centre of our whole being, and we ourselves are this centre.

Friend, all that I am, all I wish, all I might be, comes out of myself. Should not my knowledge also come out of myself?

THE ELEMENTS OF INSTRUCTION

I long sought for a common psychological origin for all these arts of instruction, because I was convinced that only through this might it be possible to discover the *form* in which the cultivating of mankind is determined through the very laws of Nature itself. It is evident this form is founded on the general organization of the mind, by means of which our understanding binds together in imagination the impressions which are received by the senses from Nature into a whole, that is into an idea, and gradually unfolds this idea clearly.

"Every line, every measure, every word," said I to myself, "is a result of understanding that is produced by ripened sense-impressions and must be regarded as a means towards the progressive clearing up of our ideas." Again, all instruction is essentially nothing but this. Its principles must therefore be derived from the immutable first form of human mental development.

Everything depends on the exact knowledge of this prototype. I therefore once more began to keep my eye on these beginning-points from which it must be derived.

"The world," said I in this reverie, "lies before our eyes like a sea of confused sense-impressions, flowing one into the other. If our development through Nature only is not sufficiently rapid and unimpeded, the business of instruction is to remove the confusion of these sense-impressions; to separate the objects one from another; to put together in imagination those that resemble or are related to each other: and in this way to make all clear to us, and by perfect clearness in these to raise in us distinct ideas. It does this when it presents these confused and blurred sense-impressions to us *one by one;* then places these separate sense-impressions in different changing positions before our eyes; and lastly, brings them into connection with the whole cycle of our previous knowledge.

"So our learning grows from confusion to definiteness; from definiteness to plainness; and from plainness to perfect clearness.

"But Nature, in her progress towards this development, is constant to the great law that makes the clearness of my knowledge depend on the nearness or distance of the object in touch with my senses. All that surrounds you reaches your senses, other things being equal, confused and difficult to make clear to yourself in proportion to its distance from your senses; on the contrary, everything that reaches your senses is distinct and easy for you to make clear and plain in proportion as it approaches your five senses.

"You are as a physical living being nothing but your five senses; consequently the clearness or mistiness of your ideas must absolutely and essentially rest upon the nearness or distance with which all external objects touch these five senses,—that is, yourself, the centre, because your ideas converge in you.

"You, yourself, are the centre of all your sense-impressions; you are also yourself an object for your sense-impressions. It is easier to make all that is within you clear and plain than all that is without you. All that you feel of yourself is in itself a *definite* sense-impression; only that which is without can be a confused sense-impression for you. It follows that the course of your knowledge, in so far as it touches yourself, is a step shorter than when it comes from something outside yourself.

"All that you know of yourself, you know clearly; all that you yourself know is in you, and in itself clear through you. It follows that this road to clear ideas is easier and safer in this direction than in any other; and among all that is clear nothing can be clearer than this principle: man's knowledge of truth comes from his knowledge of himself."

Friend! Living but vague ideas of the elements of instruction whirled about my mind for a long time in this way. So I depicted them in my Report without at that time being able to discover the unbroken connection between them and the laws of physical mechanism; and without being able to define with certainty the beginning-points from which the sequences of our views of the Art should proceed, or rather the form by which it might be possible to *determine the improvement* of mankind through his own essential nature. At last, suddenly, like a *Deus ex machina,* came the thought— The means of making clear all knowledge gained by sense-impression comes from *number, form,* and *language*. It suddenly seemed to throw a new light on what I was trying to do.

Now after my long struggle, or rather my wandering reverie, I aimed wholly and simply at finding out how a cultivated man behaves and must behave when he wishes to distinguish any object which appears misty and confused to his eyes, and gradually to make it clear to himself.

In this case he will observe three things:

1. How many and what kinds of objects are before him.
2. Their appearance, form, or outline.
3. Their names; how he may represent each of them by a sound or word.

The result of this action in such a man manifestly presupposes the following ready-formed powers:

1. The power of recognizing unlike objects according to the outline, and of representing to oneself what is contained within it.
2. That of stating the number of these objects, and representing them to himself as one or many.
3. That of representing objects, their number and form, by speech, and making them unforgettable.

I also thought *number, form,* and *language* are, together, the elementary means of instruction, because the whole sum of the external properties of any object is comprised in its outline and its number, and is brought home to my consciousness through language.

It must then be an immutable law of the Art to start from and work within this threefold principle:

1. To teach children to look upon every object that is brought before them as a unit: that is, as separated from those with which it seems connected.
2. To teach them the form of every object: that is, its *size* and *proportions*.
3. As soon as possible to make them acquainted with all the words and names descriptive of objects known to them.

And as the instruction of children should proceed from these three elementary points, it is evident that the first efforts of the Art should be directed to the primary faculties of counting, measuring, and speaking, which lie at the basis of all accurate knowledge of objects of sense. We should cultivate them with the strictest psychological Art, endeavoring to strengthen and make them strong, and to bring them, as a means of development and culture, to the highest pitch of simplicity, consistency, and harmony.

The only difficulty which struck me in the recognition of these elementary points was the question: Why are *all* qualities of things that we know through our five senses not just as much elementary points of knowledge as number, form, and names? But I soon found that all possible objects have absolutely number, form, and names; but the other characteristics, known through our five senses, are not common to all objects. I found then such an essential and definite distinction between the number, form, and names of things and their other qualities, that I could not regard other qualities as elementary points of human knowledge. Again, I found that all other qualities can be included under these elementary points; that consequently, in instructing children, all other qualities of objects must be immediately connected with form, number, and names. I saw now that through knowing the unity, form, and name of any object, my knowledge of it becomes *precise;* by gradually learning its other qualities my knowledge of it becomes *clear;* through my consciousness of all its characteristics, my knowledge of it becomes *distinct.*

Then I found, further, that all our knowledge flows from three elementary powers:

1. From the power of making sounds, the origin of language.

2. From the *indefinite, simple sensuous-power of forming images,* out of which arises the consciousness of all forms.

3. From the *definite,* no longer merely *sensuous-power of imagination,* from which must be derived consciousness of unity, and with it the power of calculation and arithmetic.

I thought, then, that the art of educating our race must be joined to the first and simplest results of these three primary powers—sound, form, and number; and that instruction in separate parts can never have a satisfactory effect upon our nature as a whole, if these three simple results of our primary powers are not recognized as the common starting-point of all instruction, determined by Nature herself. In consequence of this recognition, they must be fitted into forms which flow universally and harmoniously from the results of these three elementary powers; and which tend essentially and surely to make all instruction a steady, unbroken development of these three elementary powers, used together and considered equally important. In this way only is it possible to lead us in all three branches from vague to precise sense-impressions, from precise sense-impressions to clear images, and from clear images to distinct ideas.

Here at last I find the Art in general and essential harmony with Nature; or rather, with the prototype by which Nature makes clear to us the objects of the world in their essence and utmost simplicity. The problem is solved: *How to find a common origin of all methods and arts of instruction, and with it a form by which the development of our race might be decided through the essence of our own very nature.* The difficulties are removed of applying *mechanical laws,* which I recognize as the foundation of all human instruction, to the *form of instruction* which the experience of ages has put into the hands of mankind for the development of the race; that is, to apply them to reading, writing, arithmetic, and so on.

SENSE-IMPRESSION, THE FOUNDATION OF ALL KNOWLEDGE

Friend! When I now look back and ask myself: What have I specially done for the very being of education, I find I have fixed the highest supreme principle of instruction in the recognition of *sense-impression as the absolute foundation of all knowledge.* Apart from all *special teaching* I have sought to discover the *nature of teaching itself;* and the *prototype,* by which Nature herself has determined the instruction of our race. I find I have reduced all instruction to three elementary means; and have sought for special methods which would render the results of all instruction in these three branches absolutely certain.

Lastly, I find I have brought these three elementary means into harmony with each other; I have made instruction in all three branches in many ways harmonious not only each with itself but also with human nature; and I have brought it nearer to the course of Nature in the development of the human race.

But while I did this I found of necessity that the instruction of our country, as it is *publicly and generally* conducted *for the people,* wholly and entirely ignores sense-impression as the supreme principle of instruction; that throughout it does not take sufficient notice of the prototype, within which the instruction of our race is determined by the necessary laws of our nature itself; that it rather sacrifices the *essentials of all teaching* to the hurly burly of *isolated teaching of special things,* and kills the spirit of truth by dishing up all kinds of *broken truths;* and that it extinguishes in the human race the power of self-activity which rests upon it. I found, and it was clear as day, that this kind of instruction reduces its particular methods neither to elementary principles nor to elementary forms; that by the neglect of sense-impression as the absolute foundation of all knowledge, it is unable by any of its unconnected methods to attain the end of all instruction—clear ideas; and even to make those limited results, at which it solely aims, absolutely certain.

This [1] educational position in which at least nine men in every ten are to be found in Europe, as well as the actual quality of that instruction which they enjoy, appears almost incredible at the first glance of the subject; but it is not only historically correct, it is psychologically inevitable; it could not be otherwise. Europe, with its system of popular instruction, was bound to sink into the error, or rather insanity, that really underlay it. It rose on the one hand to a gigantic height in special arts and sciences, and lost on the other all foundations of natural teaching for the whole race. No country ever rose so high on the one side, nor sank so low on the other. Like the image of the prophet, it touches the clouds with its golden head of *special arts and sciences;*

---

[1] Even the good Lavater, caring for and honoring the positive condition of the world as nobody else did, knew and confessed this. He answered the question: What simple element can be found for the Art and particularly for the observation (*Anschauung*) of all things? *He knew none,* and it surpassed all belief how groundless the Art (of education) in Europe was.—Pestalozzi.

but popular instruction, that should be the foundation *of this golden head,* is, like the feet of this gigantic image, the *most wretched, most fragile, most good for nothing clay.*

This disproportion, ruinous for the human mind, between the advantages of the upper and the misery of the lower classes, or rather the beginning-point from which this striking disproportion in the culture of our country dates, is the invention of the art of printing. The country, in its first astonishment about this new and boundless influence, this making of word-knowledge easy, fell into a kind of dizzy, quack-like trust in the universality of its effects. This was natural in the first generation after the discovery; but that the country after so many ages still lives in the same dizzy state, and has let it grow to a soul-and-body-destroying nervous fever without feeling ill! really this could have happened in no country but ours.

But it needed another influence, interwoven of monkish, feudal, Jesuit, and government systems, in order to produce through this art *the result* it has had on Europe. With these surrounding circumstances, it is then really not only comprehensible how it came to take a positive position together with our arts and our popular instruction, but it is even clear that under given circumstances it could produce no *inferior* art but also no *better* instruction than it has actually produced. It is quite clear how it was *forced* to narrow the five senses of the country, and so to bind particularly that instrument of sense-impression, the eye, to the heathen altar of the new learning, letters and books. I might almost say it was forced to make this universal instrument of knowledge a mere letter-eye, and us mere letter-men.

The Reformation (by the weakening of its original spirit

and the necessary resulting deification of dead forms and thoughts) completed what the art of printing began. Without putting its heart under the obvious stupidity of a monkish or feudal world, it has opened its mouth generally only to express abstract ideas. This still more increased the inner atrophy of the world, making its men letter-beings; and brought it to such a point that the errors of this condition cannot be dissolved by progress in truth, love, and faith; but on the contrary, they can only be strengthened, while they seem to be dissolved, by the still more dangerous errors of infidelity, indifference, and lawlessness.

As a devastating flood, checked in its career by a fallen rock, takes a new course and spreads its devastation from generation to generation, so European popular education, having once forsaken the even road of sense-impression, owing to the influence of these two great events, has taken generally a baseless, visionary course, increasing its human devastation year by year, from generation to generation.

Now after ages it has culminated in the general *word-twisting* of our knowledge. This has led to the word-twisting of infidelity. This profound vice of word and dream is in no way fitted to raise us to the still wisdom of faith and love, but on the contrary to lead as to the word-twisting of sham and superstition and its indifference and hardness. In any case it is undeniable that this devouring word and book nature of our culture has brought us to this—we cannot any longer remain as we are.

It could not be otherwise. Since we have contrived with deeply founded art and still more deeply founded measures for supporting error, to rob our knowledge and our methods of instruction of all sense-impression, and ourselves of all power of gaining sense-impressions, the gilded, giddy pate of our culture could not possibly stand on any feet but those on which it does actually stand. Nothing else was possible. The drifting haphazard methods of our culture could in no subject attain the final end of public instruction, *clear ideas,* and *perfect facility* in what is essentially necessary for the people to know and to learn of all these subjects.

Even the best of these methods, the abundant aids for teaching arithmetic (mathematics) and grammar must under these circumstances lose power, because without finding any other foundation for all instruction they have neglected sense-impression. So these means of instruction, word, number, and form, not being sufficiently subordinated to the one only foundation of all knowledge, sense-impression, must necessarily mislead our generation to elaborate these means of instruction unequally, superficially, and aimlessly, in the midst of error and deception; and by this elaboration, weaken our inmost powers, rather than strengthen and cultivate them. We become necessarily degraded to *lies* and *folly,* and branded as miserable, weak, unobservant, wordy babblers, by the very same powers and the very same organism [1] with which the Art, holding the hand of Nature, might raise us up to *truth and wisdom....*

SENSE-IMPRESSION, LANGUAGE AND CLEARNESS OF IDEAS

Friend! sense-impression, considered as the point at which all instruction begins, must be differentiated from the art of sense-impression (*Anschauung*) which teaches us the relations of all forms. Sense-impression, as the common foun-

---

[1] Edition I: Mechanism.

65

dation of all three elementary means of instruction, must come as long before the art of sense-impression as it comes before the arts of reckoning and speaking. If we consider sense-impression as opposed to the art of sense-impression (*Anschauung*) separately and by itself, it is nothing but the presence of *the external object before the senses* which rouses a consciousness of the impression made by it. With it Nature begins all instruction. The infant enjoys it, the mother gives it him.

But the Art has done nothing here to keep equal pace with Nature. In vain that most beautiful spectacle, the mother showing the world to her infant, was presented to its eyes; *the Art has done nothing, has verily done nothing for the people,* in connection with this spectacle.

Dear Gessner, I will here quote for you the passage that expressed this feeling about our Art more than a year ago.

"From the moment that a mother takes a child upon her lap, she teaches him. She brings nearer to his senses what nature has scattered afar off over large areas and in confusion, and makes the action of receiving sense-impressions, and the knowledge derived from them, easy, pleasant, and delightful to him.

"The mother, weak and untrained, follows Nature without help or guidance, and knows not what she is doing. She does not intend to teach; she intends only to quiet the child, to occupy him. But nevertheless in her pure simplicity she follows the high course of Nature without knowing what *Nature* does through *her;* and Nature does very much through her. In this way she opens the world to the child. She makes him ready to use his senses, and prepares for the early development of his attention and power of observation.

HOW GERTRUDE TEACHES HER CHILDREN

"Now if this high course of Nature were used; if that were connected with it which might be connected with it; if the helping Art could make it possible to the mother's heart to go on with what she does instinctively for the infant, wisely and freely with the growing child; if, too, the heart (and disposition) of the father were also used for this purpose; and if the helping Art made it possible for him to link with the disposition and circumstances of the child all the activities he needs, in order by good management of his most important affairs to attain inner content with himself throughout his life, how easy would it be to assist in raising our race and every individual man in any position whatever, even amid the difficulties of unfavorable circumstances, and amid all the evils of unhappy times, and secure him a still, calm, peaceful life. O God! What would be gained for men. But we are not yet so far advanced as the Appenzell woman, who in the first weeks of her child's life hangs a large many-colored paper bird over his cradle, and in this way clearly shows the point at which the Art should begin to bring the objects of Nature firmly to the child's clear consciousness."

Dear friend! Whoever has seen how the two- and three-weeks old child stretches hands and feet towards this bird, and considers how easy it would be for the Art to lay a foundation for actual sense-impressions of all objects of Art and Nature in the child by a series of such visible representations, which may then be made gradually more distinct and extended—whoever considers all this and then does not feel how we have wasted our time on Gothic monkish educational rubbish, until it has become hateful to us—truly cakes and ale are wasted on him.

To me the Appenzell bird, like the ox to the Egyptians, is a holy thing, and I have done everything to begin my instruction at the same point as the Appenzell woman. I go further. Neither at the first point nor in the whole series of means of teaching do I leave to chance what nature, circumstance, or mother-love may present to the sense of the child before he can speak. I have done all I could to make it possible, by omitting accidental characteristics, to bring the essentials of knowledge gained by sense-impression to the child's senses before that age, and to make the conscious impressions he receives unforgettable.

The first *course in the Mother's Book* is nothing but an attempt to raise sense-impression itself to an art, and to lead the children by all three elementary divisions of knowledge, *form, number,* and *words,* to a comprehensive consciousness of all sense-impressions, the more definite concepts of which will constitute the foundation of their later knowledge.

This book will contain not only representations of those objects most necessary for us to know, but also material for a continuous series of such objects as are fit, at the first sense-impression, to rouse a feeling in the children of their manifold relationships and similarities.

In this respect the Spelling Book does the same thing as the Mother's Book. Simply bringing sounds *to the ear* and rousing a consciousness of the impression made *through the hearing,* is as much *sense-impression* for the child as putting objects *before his eye,* and rousing a consciousness of the impression made *through the sense of sight.* Founded on this, I have so arranged the Spelling Book that its first course is nothing but *simple sense-impression;* that is, it rests simply on the effort to bring the whole series of sounds that must afterwards serve as the foundation of language *to the child's sense of hearing,* and to make the impression made by them permanent *at exactly the same age* at which in the Mother's Book I bring before his sense of sight the visible objects of the world, the clear perception of which must be the foundation of his future knowledge.

This same principle, of raising sense-impression to an art, has a place too in our third elementary means of knowledge. Number in itself, without a foundation of sense-impression, is a delusive phantom of an idea, which our imagination certainly holds in a dreamy fashion, but which our reason cannot grasp firmly as a truth. The child must learn to know rightly the inner nature of every form in which the relations of number may appear, before he is in a position to comprehend one of these forms as the foundation of a clear consciousness of few or many. Therefore in the Mother's Book I have impressed the first ten numbers on the child's senses (*Anschauung*) even at this age in many ways, by fingers, claws, leaves, dots, and also as triangle, square, octagon, etc.

After I have done this in all three branches, and have made sense-impression the absolute foundation of all actual knowledge, I again raise sense-impression in all three subjects to the art of sense-impression (*Anschauung*), that is, a power of considering all objects of sense-impression as *objects for the exercise of my judgment and my skill.* (*Fertigkeit*)

In this way I lead the child, with the first elementary means of knowledge, *Form.* After I have made him acquainted in the Mother's Book with manifold sense-impressions of the objects and their names, I lead him to the A B C of the art of sense-impression (*Anschauung*). By this he is put in a position to give an account of the form of objects, which he *distinguished* in the Mother's Book, but did not *clearly* know. This book will enable the child to form clear ideas on the forms of all things by their relation to the square, and in this way to find a whole series of means within the compass of subjects of instruction, by which he may rise from vague sense-impressions to clear ideas.

With regard to the second primary means of knowledge, *Number*, I go on in the same way. After I have tried by the Mother's Book to make the child clearly conscious, before he can speak, of the ideas of *the first ten numbers*, I try to teach him these expressions for few or many things, by gradually adding *one unit to another*, and making him know the nature of *two*, and then of *three*, and so on. And thus I bring the beginning of all reckoning to the clearest sense-impression of the child, and at the same time make him unforgettably familiar with the expressions which stand for them.

Thus I bring the beginnings of arithmetic in general into sequences which are nothing but a psychological, certain and unbroken march onwards from deeply impressed judgments, resting on sense-impression, to a little additional new sense-impression, but mounting only from 1 to 2 and from 2 to 3. The result of this course, ascertained by experience, is that when the children have wholly understood the beginning of any kind of calculation, they are able to go on without further help.

It is generally to be noticed with respect to this manner of teaching that it tends to make the principles of each subject so evident to the children that they can complete every step by their learning, so that in every case they may be absolutely considered (and used) as teachers of their younger brothers and sisters, as far as they have gone themselves.

The most important thing that I have done to simplify and illustrate number teaching is this: I not only bring the consciousness of the truth within all relations of numbers to the child, by means of sense-impression; but I unite this truth of sense-impression with the truth of the science of magnitudes, and have set up the square as the common foundation of the art of sense-impression and of arithmetic.

The third primary means of knowledge, *Speech,* considered as an application of my principles, is capable of the greatest extension.

If knowledge of form and number should precede speech (and this last must partly arise from the first two), it follows that the progress of grammar is quicker than that of the art of sense-impression (*Anschauung*) and arithmetic. The impression made on the senses (*Anschauung*) by form and number *precedes* the art of *speech,* but the art of sense-impression and arithmetic *comes after* the *art of speech* (*grammar*). The great peculiarity and highest characteristic of our nature, *Language,* begins in the power of making sounds. It becomes gradually developed by improving *sounds* to *articulate words;* and from *articulate words* to *language.*

Nature needed ages to raise our race to perfect power of speech, yet we learn this art, for which Nature in respect to this subject needed ages, in a few months. In teaching our children to speak we must then follow exactly the same course .that Nature followed with the human race. We dare not do otherwise. And she unquestionably began with sense-impression. Even the simplest sound by which man strove to express the impression that an object made on him, was an expression of a sense-impression.

The speech of my race was long only a *power of mimicry and of making sounds* that imitated the tones of living and lifeless nature. From *mimicry* and *sound-making* they came to *hieroglyphics* and *separate words,* and for long they gave *special* objects *special* names. This condition of language is sublimely described in the first book of Moses, ii. 19, 20: "The Lord God brought to Adam all the beasts of the earth, and all the birds under heaven, that he might *look upon them* and *name* them. And Adam gave every beast his name."

From this point speech gradually went further. Men first *observed* the striking differences in the objects that they *named.* Then they came to name properties; and then to name the differences in the *actions* and *forces* of objects. Much later the art developed of *making single words mean much,* unity, plurality, size, many or few, form and number, and at last to express clearly all variations and properties of an object which were produced by changes of time and place, by modifying the form and by joining words together.

In all these stages, speech was to the race a *means* produced by art, not only of *representing* the actual process of making manifold ideas (*Intuitionen*) clear by the power of sound, but also of *making impressions unforgettable.*

Language-teaching is, then, in its nature, nothing but a collection of psychological means of expressing impressions (feelings and thoughts); and of making all their modifications that would be else *fleeting* and *incommunicable, last-*

ing and *communicable* by uniting them to words. . . .

The course of Nature in the development of our race is unchangeable. There are and can be no *two good* methods of instruction in this respect. There is but *one*—and this is the one that rests entirely upon the eternal laws of Nature. But of *bad* methods there are *infinitely many;* and the badness of every one *increases* in proportion as it *deviates from the law of Nature,* and *decreases* in proportion as *it approaches* to following these laws.

I well know that this one good method is neither in my hands nor in any other man's; that we can only approach it. But its completion, its perfection must be the aim of him who would found human instruction upon truth, and thereby content human nature and satisfy its natural claims. From this point of view, I declare I pursue this method of instruction with all the powers that are in my hands. I have one rule for judging my own action, as well as the actions of all those who strive for this end—*by their fruits ye shall know them.* Human power, mother-wit, and common sense are to me the only evidence of the inner worth of any kind of instruction. Any method that brands the brow of the learner with the stamp of completely stifled natural powers and the want of common sense and mother-wit, is condemned by me, whatever other advantages it may have. I do not deny that even *such* methods may produce good tailors, shoemakers, tradesmen, and soldiers; but I do deny that they can produce a tailor or a tradesman who is *a man* in the highest sense of the word.

Oh, if men would only comprehend that the aim of all instruction is, and can be, nothing but the development of human nature, by the harmonious cultivation of its powers and talents and the promotion of manliness of life. Oh, if they would only ask themselves, at every step in their methods of education and instruction, "Does it further this end?"

I will now again consider the influence of clear ideas upon the essential development of humanity. *Clear* ideas to the child are only *those to which his experience can bring no more clearness*. This principle settles, first, the order of the powers and faculties to be developed, by which the *clearness* of all ideas can gradually be arrived at; secondly, the *order* of *objects* by which exercises in definitions can be begun and carried on with the children; lastly, the *exact time* at which definitions of *any kind* contain real truth for the child.

It is evident that *clear ideas* must be worked out or cultivated in the child by teaching, before we can take for granted that he is *able* to understand the result of such training—the clear idea, or rather its statement in words.

The way to *clear ideas* depends on making all objects clear to the reason in their proper order. This order again rests on the *harmony* of all the arts, by which a child is enabled to express himself clearly about the properties of all things, particularly about the measure, number, and form of any object. In this way, and no other, can the child be led to a comprehensive knowledge of the whole nature of any object, and become capable of defining it; that is, of stating in words its whole nature, with the utmost precision and brevity. All definitions—that is, all such clear statements in words of the nature of any object—contain essential truth for the child only so far as he has a clear, vivid background of sense-impression of the object. Where thorough clearness in the sense-impression of the object to be defined is wanting, he only learns to play with words; to deceive himself; and to believe blindly in words whose sounds convey no idea to him, or give him no other thought than that he has just given out a sound.

HINC ILLAE LACRYMAE

In rainy weather toadstools grow fast on every dungheap; and in the same way definitions not founded on sense-impression produce, just as quickly, a fungus-like wisdom, which dies just as quickly in the sunlight, and which looks upon the clear sky as poison to it. The baseless, wordy show of such baseless wisdom produces men who believe they have reached the end in all subjects, because their life is a tiresome babble about this end. They have never reached it, never pursued it, because all their life it has not had that attractive charm for their observing powers (*Anschauung*) which is generally necessary to produce a manly effort.

Our generation is full of such men. They lie sick of a kind of wisdom that leads us *pro forma* to the goal of knowledge, like cripples on the race course, without being able to make this goal their goal until their feet are cured. The power of describing generally precedes definition. I can describe what is quite clear to me, but I cannot on that account define it. That is, I can say exactly what its properties are but not what it is. I only know the object, the individual; I cannot yet point out its relations or its kind. Of that which is not clear to me, I cannot say exactly what its properties are, let alone what it is. I cannot describe it, much less define it. When a third person, to whom the matter is clear, puts words into my mouth with which he makes it clear to *people in his own condition,* it is not on that account clear to me, but it is and will remain his clear thing, not mine, inasmuch as the words of another cannot be for me what they are to him—the exact expression of his own idea, which is to him perfectly clear.

This purpose of leading men, with psychological art and according to the laws of their physical mechanism, to clear ideas, and to their expression, definitions, demands a gradation of statements about the physical world before definitions. This gradation proceeds from sense-impressions of separate objects to their names, from their names to determining their characteristics, that is the power of describing; and from the power of describing to the power of *specializing,* that is, of defining. Wisdom in guiding sense-impression is obviously the beginning-point on which this chain of means for attaining clear ideas must depend; and it is obvious that the final fruit, the end of all instruction, the clearness of all ideas, depends essentially on the complete power of its first germination.

Wherever in the whole circle of all-working Nature anything is imperfect in the germ, there it has lost the power of becoming perfect in its complete ripeness. Everything that is imperfect in the germ will be crippled in its growth, in the outward development of its parts. This is as true of the products of your mind as of the products of your garden. It is as true of the results of a single idea gained by sense-impression, as it is certain of the condition of a grown cabbage.

The most important means of preventing confusion, inconsequence, and superficiality in human education, rests principally on care on making the first sense-impression of *things most essential* for us to know, as clear, correct, and comprehensive as possible, when they are first brought before our senses, for contemplation (*Anschauung*). Even at the infant's cradle we must begin to take the training of our race out of the hands of blind, sportive Nature, and put it into the hands of that better power which the experience of ages has taught us to abstract from the eternal laws of our nature.

You must generally distinguish between the laws of Nature and her course; that is, her single workings, and statements about those workings. In her laws she is eternal truth, and for us, the eternal standard of all truth; but in her modifications, in which her laws apply to every individual and to every case, her truth does not satisfy and content our race. The positive truth of the condition and circumstances of any individual case claims the same equal right of necessity, by virtue of eternal laws, as the common law of human nature itself. Consequently, the claim of necessity of both laws must be brought into harmony, if they are to work satisfactorily on men. Care for this union is essential for our race. The accidental is, by its existence and its consequences, as necessary as the eternal and unchangeable; but the accidental must, from its very existence and its inevitable consequences, be brought into harmony with the eternal and unchangeable in human nature by means of the freedom of the human will.

Nature, on which the inevitable laws of the existence and consequences of the accidental are based, seems only devoted to the whole, and is careless of the individual that she is affecting externally. On this side she is blind; and being blind, she is not the Nature that comes or can come into harmony with the seeing, spiritual, moral nature of men. On the contrary, it is only simple and moral nature that is able to bring itself into harmony with the physical—and that can, and ought to do so.

The laws of our senses, by virtue of the essential claims of our nature, must be subordinated to the laws of our moral and spiritual life. Without this subordination it is impossible that the physical part of our nature can ever influence the actual final result of our education, the production of manliness. Man will become man only through his inner and spiritual life. He becomes through it independent, free, and contented. Mere physical Nature leads him not hither. She is in her very nature blind; her ways are ways of darkness and death. Therefore the education and training of our race must be taken out of the hands of blind sensuous Nature, and the influence of her darkness and death, and put into the hands of our moral and spiritual being, and its divine, eternal, inner light and truth.

All, all that you carelessly leave to outer blind Nature sinks. That is true of lifeless nature as of living. Wherever you carelessly leave the earth to Nature, it bears weeds and thistles. Wherever you leave the education of your race to her, she goes no further than a confused impression on the senses that is not adapted to your power of comprehension, nor to that of your child in the way that is needed for the best instruction.

In order to lead a child in the most certain way to correct and perfect knowledge of a tree or plant, it is not by any means the best way to turn him without care into a wood or meadow where trees and plants of all kinds grow together. Neither trees nor plants here come before his eyes in such a manner as is calculated to make him observe their nature and relationships, and to prepare for a general knowledge of their subject by the first impression. In order to lead your child by the shortest way to the end of instruction, clear ideas, you must with great care first put before his eyes, visibly and distinctly, those objects (in every branch of learning) which bear the most essential characteristics of the branch to which this object belongs, and which are therefore fitted to strike the eye with the essential nature rather than the variable qualities. If you neglect this, you lead the child at the very first glance to look upon the accidental qualities as essential, and in this at least to delay the knowledge of truth, and miss the shortest road of rising from misty sense-impressions to clear ideas.

But if this error in your method of instruction is avoided, if the sequences of subjects in all branches of your instruction are brought to the child's sense-impression so arranged from the very beginning that at the very first observation (*Anschauung*) the impression of the essential nature of an object begins to overpower the impression of its qualities, the child learns from the very first to subordinate the accidental properties of an object to its essential nature. He is undoubtedly moving on the safe path, in which his power develops daily, of connecting in the simplest manner all accidental qualities with his full consciousness of the essential nature of all objects and their inner truth, and so to read all Nature as an open book.

As a child, left to itself, peeping into the world without understanding, sinks daily from error to error, through the confusion of separate scraps of knowledge which he has found while so groping; so, on the contrary, a child who is led on this road from his cradle rises gaily from truth to truth. All that exists, or at least all that comes within the range of his experience, unites itself clearly and comprehensively with the power already existing in him, and there is no error behind his views. No bias to any kind of error has been artificially and methodically organized in him, and the *nihil admirari,* which has hitherto been considered the privilege of old age, becomes, thanks to this training, the portion of innocence and youth. Having arrived at this, if he possesses fair average abilities the child will necessarily reach the final goal of instruction, clear ideas—it matters little for the time being whether these lead him to the conclusion that we know nothing, or that we understand everything. . . .

PRACTICAL SKILL; ITS IMPORTANCE AND ITS CULTIVATION

In my experimental inquiries into the subject, I started from no positive notion of teaching—I had *none*—I ask myself simply, "What would you do, if you wished to produce in a single child, all the *knowledge* and *ability* that it needs, in order *by wise care of its essential concerns to attain to inward content?"*

But I see now that in the whole series of my letters to you, I have only considered the first portion of the subject, the training of the child's *judgment* and *knowledge;* but not the training of his *activities,* so far as these are not especially activities brought out by instruction (in knowledge and science). And yet the activities that a man needs to attain inner content by their possession are not actually limited to the few subjects that the nature of instruction forced me to touch upon.

I cannot leave these gaps untouched. Perhaps the most fearful gift that a fiendish spirit has made to this age is *knowledge without power of doing and insight without that power of exertion or of overcoming* that makes it possible and easy for our life to be in harmony with our inmost nature.

Man! needing much and desiring all, thou must to satisfy thy wants and wishes *know* and *think*, but for this thou must also (*can* and) *do*. And knowing and doing are so closely connected that if one ceases the other ceases with it. But there can be this harmony between thy life and thy inmost nature only if the *powers of doing* (without which it is impossible to satisfy thy wishes and wants) are cultivated in thee with just the same art, and raised to the same degree of perfection, as thy insight into the objects of thy wants and wishes. The cultivation of these activities rests then on the same organic laws as the cultivation of knowledge.

The organism of Nature is one and the same in the living plant; in the animal, whose nature is merely physical; and in man, whose nature is also physical, but who possesses will. In the threefold results which Nature is capable of producing in me, she is always the same. Her laws work either physically upon my physical nature, in the same manner as upon animals generally; or, secondly, they work upon me so far as they determine the *sensuous basis of my judgment and will*. In this respect they are the sensuous basis of my opinions, my inclinations, and my resolutions. Thirdly, they work upon me so far as *they make me capable of that practical skill*, the need of which I *feel* through my instinct, I *recognize* through my insight, and the learning of which I *command* through my will. But in this respect also, the Art must take the cultivation of our race out of the hands of Nature, or rather from her accidental attitude towards each individual, in order to put it in the hands of knowledge, power, and methods, which she has taught us for ages to the advantage of the race. . . .

All ability, on the possession of which depend all the powers of knowing and doing that are required by an educated mind and a noble heart, comes as little of itself as the *intelligence* and *knowledge* that man needs for it. As the cultivation of mental powers and faculties presupposes a psychologically arranged gradation of means, adapted to human nature, so the cultivation of the faculties which these powers of doing presuppose, rests on the deep-rooted mechanism of an A B C of *Art;* that is on universal laws of the Art, by following which the children may be educated by a series of exercises, proceeding gradually from the simplest to the most complicated. These must result, with physical certainty, in obtaining for them a daily increasing facility in all that they need for their education.

But this A B C is anything but *found.* It is quite natural that we seldom find anything that nobody looks for. But if we would seek it with all the earnestness with which we are wont to seek any small advantage in the money-market, it would be easy to find, and when found would be a great blessing to mankind. It must start from the simplest manifestations of physical powers, which contain the foundations of the most complicated human practical ability. Striking and carrying, thrusting and throwing, drawing and turning, encircling and swinging, etc., are extremely simple expressions of our physical powers. In themselves essentially different, they contain, all together and each separately, the foundation of all possible actions, even the most complicated, on which human callings depend. Therefore, it is obvious that the A B C of actions must start altogether from early psychologically arranged exercises in these actions, all and each. This A B C of limb exercise must, naturally, be brought into harmony with the A B C of sense exercises, and with all the mechanical practice in thinking, and with exercises in form and number-teaching.

But as we are far behind the Appenzell woman and her paper bird in the A B C of *Anschauung,* so are we far behind the greatest barbarians in the A B C of actions (gymnastics) and their skill in striking and throwing, thrusting and dragging.

We want a graduated series of exercises, from their simplest beginning to their highest perfection; that is, to the utmost delicacy of nerve power which enables us to perform with certainty and in a hundred different ways the actions of thrusting and parrying, swinging and throwing. We want, too, actions exercising hand and foot in opposite as well as in the same directions. All these, as far as popular instruction is concerned, are castles in the air. The ground is clear. We have spelling schools, writing schools, catechism (Heidelberger) schools only, and we want—*men's schools.*

But these can be of no use to those whose whole idea is to keep things as they are, to the jobbery and injustice that are so readily maintained by this idea; nor to the nervous state of the gentry whose interests are involved in this contemptible state of *laissez-faire.* (But I almost forget the point at which I began.)

The mechanism of activities takes the same course as that of knowledge, and its foundations with regard to self-education are perhaps still more far-reaching. In order to *be able,* you must *act;* in order to *know,* you must, in many cases, keep *passive;* you can only see and hear. Hence in relation to your activities you are not only the centre of their cultivation, but in many cases you determine their ultimate use—always within the laws of the physical mechanism. As in the infinite range of lifeless nature, its situation, needs, and relations have determined the special characteristics of every object; so in the infinite range of living nature that produces the development of your faculties, your situation, needs, and relations determine the sort of power that you specially need.

These considerations throw light on the mode of developing our activities, and also on the character of the activities when developed. Every influence that in the development of our powers and activities turns us away from the centre point on which rests the personal responsibility of everything that man is bound throughout his life to do, to bear, to attend and provide for, must be regarded as an influence opposed to wise manly education. Every influence leading us to apply our powers and activities in a way that turns us away from this central point, and thus weakens or robs the activities of the special character which our duty towards ourselves requires of us, or puts us out of accord with them, or in some way or other makes us incapable of serving our fellow-men or our country, must be regarded as a deviation from the laws of nature, from the harmony with myself and my surroundings. Therefore it is a hindrance to my self-culture, to the training for my calling, and to my sense of duty. It is a delusive and self-destructive deviation from the pure and beautiful dependence of my relations in life on my real character.

Every kind of instruction or education, every kind of life, every use of our trained powers and talents in life, which bears in itself the seeds of such discord between our education and our actions, and the real character of our being, our relations and our duties, must be guarded against by all fathers and mothers who have their children's life-long peace of mind at heart; for we must seek the sources of the infinite evil of our baseless *sham-enlightenment,* and the misery of our *masquerade revolution,* in errors of this kind; since both find a place alike in the instruction and in the life of our educated and uneducated people.

The necessity of great care for the psychological manner of developing and cultivating our powers of doing, as well as the psychological training for the development of our power of knowing, is obvious. This psychological training for the development of our powers of knowing is based on an A B C of *Anschauung,* and must lead the child by this fundamental clue to the fullest purity of clear ideas. For the cultivation of the activities, on which the sense-foundation of our *virtue* rests, we must seek for an A B C for developing this power; and on its lines a sense-cultivation, a physical dexterity of those powers and activities which are needed for the life-duties of our race, which we must recognize as *leading strings in the nursery of virtue,* until our senses, ennobled by this training, need the leading-strings no longer.

In this way can be developed a general kind of education, suitable to the human race, for training those practical abilities which are necessary for the fulfilment of the duties of life. It goes from *complete power of doing to the recognition of law,* just as the education of intelligence goes from *complete sense-impression to clear ideas,* and from these to their expression in words, to definitions.

Therefore it is that as *definitions before sense-impression* lead men to presumptuous chatter, so word-teachings about virtue and faith, preceding the realities of living sense-impressions, lead men astray to similar confusion about them. It is undeniable that the presumption of these confusions, by virtue of the inner profanity and impurity that lie at the bottom of all presumption, leads even the virtuous faithful generally to the common vice of presumption. I believe also (experience speaks loudly on this view, and it must be so) that gaps in the early sense-cultivation of virtue have the same consequences as gaps in the early sense-cultivation of knowledge. . . .

MORAL EDUCATION

Friend! As I said, it would have led me too far to enter into details of the principles and laws upon which the cultivation of the practical abilities in life depend. But I will not end my letters without touching on the keystone of my whole system, namely this question— How is religious feeling connected with these principles which I have accepted as generally true for the development of the human race?

Here also I seek the solution of my problem in myself, and I ask: How is the idea of God germinated in my soul? How comes it that I believe in God, that I throw myself in His arms, and feel blessed when I love Him, trust Him, thank Him, follow Him?

HOW GERTRUDE TEACHES HER CHILDREN

I soon see that the feelings of love, trust, gratitude, and readiness to obey, must be developed in me before I can apply them to God. I must love men, trust men, thank men, and obey men before I can aspire to love, thank, trust, and obey God. For whoso loveth not his brother whom he hath seen, how can he love God whom he hath not seen?

Then I ask myself: How do I come to love, trust, thank, and obey men? How come those feelings in my nature on which human love, human gratitude, human confidence rest, and those activities by which obedience is formed? And I find: *That they have their chief source in the relations that exist between the baby and his mother.*

The mother is forced by the power of animal instinct to tend her child, feed him, protect and please him. She does this. She satisfies his wants, she removes anything unpleasant, she comes to the help of his helplessness. The child is cared for, is pleased. *The germ of love is developed in him.*

Now put an object that he has never seen before his eyes; he is astonished, frightened; he cries. The mother presses him to her bosom, dandles him, and diverts him. He leaves off crying, but his eyes are still wet. The object appears again. The mother takes him into her sheltering arms and smiles at him again. Now he weeps no more. He returns his mother's smile with clear and unclouded eyes. *The germ of trust is developed in him.*

The mother hastens to his cradle at his every need. She is there at the hour of hunger, she gives him drink in the hour of thirst. When he hears her step he is quiet; when he sees her he stretches out his hands. His eye is cast on her breast. He is satisfied. Mother, and being satisfied, are one and the same thought to him. *He is grateful.*

The germs of love, trust, and gratitude soon grow. The child knows his mother's step; he smiles at her shadow. He loves those who are like her; a creature like his mother is a good creature to him. He smiles at his mother's face, at all human faces; he loves those who are dear to his mother. Whom his mother embraces, he embraces; whom his mother kisses, he kisses too. *The germ of human love, of brotherly love is developed in him.*

Obedience in its origin is an activity whose driving-wheel is opposed to the first inclinations of animal nature. Its cultivation rests on art. It is not a simple result of pure instinct, but it is closely connected with it. Its first stage is distinctly instinctive. As *want* precedes love, *nourishment* gratitude, and *care* trust, so *passionate desire* precedes obedience. The child screams before he waits; he is impatient before he obeys. Patience is developed before obedience; he become obedient only through patience. The first manifestations of this virtue are simply passive; they arise generally from a consciousness of hard necessity. But this, too, is first developed on the mother's lap. The child must wait until she opens her breast to him; he must wait until she takes him up. *Active* obedience develops much later, and later still the consciousness that it is good for him to obey his mother.

The development of the human race begins in a strong passionate desire for the satisfaction of physical wants. The mother's breast stills the first storm of physical needs and creates *love;* soon after *fear* is developed. The mother's arm stills *fear.* These actions produce the *union* of the feelings of love and trust, and develop the first germ of *gratitude.*

Nature is inflexible towards the passionate child. He

beats wood and stone; Nature is inflexible, and the child *ceases to beat* wood and stone. Now the mother is inflexible towards his irregular desires. He rages and roars—she is still inflexible. He *leaves off crying;* he becomes accustomed to subject his will to hers. *The first germs of patience, the first germs of obedience are developed.*

Obedience and love, gratitude and trust united, develop the first germ of conscience, the first faint shadow of the feeling that *it is not right* to rage against the loving mother; the first faint shadow of the feeling that the mother is not in the world *altogether for his sake;* the first faint shadow of a feeling that everything in the world is not altogether for his sake; and with it is also germinated the feeling that *he himself* is not in the world for *his own sake* only. The first shadow of duty and right is in the germ.

These are the first principles of moral self-development, which are unfolded by the natural relations between mother and child. But in them lies the whole essence of the natural germ of that state of mind which is peculiar to human dependence on the Author of our being. That is, the germ of all feelings of dependence on God, through faith, is in its essence the same germ which is produced by the infant's dependence on its mother. The manner in which these feelings develop is one and the same.

In both, the infant hears, believes, follows; but in both at this time it *knows* not what it believes and *what it does.* Meanwhile, at this time, the *first grounds* of its faith and actions begin to vanish. Growing independence makes the child let go his mother's hand. He begins to become conscious of his own personality, and a secret thought unfolds itself in his heart— *"I no longer need my mother."* She reads the growing thought in his eyes; she presses her darling more firmly to her heart, and says, in a voice he has not yet heard: "Child, there is a God whom thou needest, who taketh thee in His arms when thou needest me no longer, when I can shelter thee no more. There is a God who prepares joy and happiness for thee when I can no more give them thee."

Then an inexpressible something rises in the child's heart, a holy feeling, a desire for faith, that raises him above himself. He rejoices in the name of God as soon as he hears his mother speak it. The feelings of love, gratitude, and trust that were developed at her bosom, extend and embrace God as father, God as mother. The practice of obedience has a wider field. The child, who believes from this time forwards in the eye of God as in the eye of his mother, does right now for *God's sake,* as he formerly did right for his *mother's sake.*

Here, in this first attempt of the mother's innocence and the mother's heart to *unite the first feeling of independence with the newly developed feeling of morality through the inclination to faith in God,* the foundations are disclosed on which education and instruction must cast their eyes if they would aim with certainty at ennobling us.

As the first germination of love, gratitude, trust, and obedience was a simple result of the *coincidence of instinctive feelings* between mother and child, so the *further development* of these germinated feelings is a *high human art.* But it is an art the threads of which will be *lost* in your hands if for one moment you lose sight of the origin from which the web springs. The danger of this loss to the child is great, and comes early. He lisps his mother's name, he loves, thanks, trusts, and follows. He lisps the name of God, he loves, thanks, trusts, and follows. But the motives of gratitude, love, and trust vanish with the first appearance of the idea: *He needs his mother no more.* The world that now surrounds him appears to him in a new light, and entices him with its pleasure, saying, *"You are mine now."*

The child cannot but hear this voice. The instinct of the infant is quenched in him; the instinct of *growing powers take its place;* and the germ of morality, *in so far as it begins in feelings that are proper to the infant,* suddenly withers up, and must wither if at this moment no one attaches to the golden spindle of creation the thread of his life that is the first throbbing of the higher feelings of his moral nature.

Mother, mother! the world is now beginning to wean your child from your heart; and if at this moment no one connects his nobler nature with the new revelation of the world of sense, it is all over. Mother, mother! your child is torn from your heart. The new world becomes his mother, *the new world* becomes his god, *sensual pleasure* becomes his god, *self-will* becomes his god.

Mother, mother! he has lost you, he has lost God, he has lost himself. The touch of love is quenched for him. The germ of self-respect is dead within him. He is going towards destruction, striving only after sensual enjoyment.

Mankind, mankind! now with this transition when the feelings of infancy vanish in the first consciousness of the charm of the world, independent of the mother—now when the ground in which the noblest feelings of nature germinate begins for the first time to tremble under the child's feet; now when the mother begins to be no more what she once was to her child; now when the germ of trust in the new aspect of the world is developed in him, and the charm of this new manifestation begins to *stifle and devour* his trust in his mother, who is no more what she once was to him, and with it his trust in an unseen and unknown God—as the wild web of tangled roots of the poisonous plant stifle and devour the finer web of roots of the noblest plants—now, mankind! now at this moment of transition between the feelings of trust in mother and God, and those of trust in the new aspect of the world and all that therein is—now at this parting place, you should use all your art and all your power to keep the feelings of love, gratitude, trust, and obedience pure in your child.

God is in these feelings, and the whole power of your moral life is intrinsically connected with their preservation.

Mankind! at this time when the physical causes of the germination of these feelings in the infant cease, your Art should do everything to bring to hand *new methods of stimulating them, and to let the attractions of the world come before the mind of your growing child only in connection with them.*

Now for the first time you *cannot trust Nature,* but must *do everything* to *take* the reins out of her blind *hands* and put them into the hands of principles and powers in which the experience of ages has put them. The world that appears before the child's eyes is not God's first creation; it is a world spoilt alike for the innocent enjoyment of the senses and for the feelings of his inner nature. It is a world full of war for the means of gratifying selfishness, full of contradiction, full of violence, presumption, lying, and deceit.

HOW GERTRUDE TEACHES HER CHILDREN

Not God's first creation but *this* world decoys the child to the giddy dance of the whirlpool of the abyss whose depths are the home of lovelessness and moral death. Not God's creation, but the brute force and art of bringing about its own ruin, is what *this* world puts before the child's eyes.

Poor child! your dwelling-room is your world; but your father is bound to his workshop, your mother is vexed to-day, has company to-morrow, and has whims the next day. You are bored; you ask questions; your nurse will not answer. You want to go out; you may not. Now you quarrel with your sister about a toy.—Poor child! what a miserable, heartless, heart-corrupting thing your world is! But is it anything more when you drive about in a gilded carriage under shady trees? Your guide deceives your mother. You suffer less, but you become worse than all sufferers. What have you gained? Your world is become a heavier load to you than any pain.

This world is so rocked to sleep in the ruin of a perverse and oppressive opposition to the laws of Nature that it has no mind for being the means of preserving purity in the heart of man; on the contrary, it is as careless at the critical moment of the innocence of our race as a heartless second wife of her step-child: a carelessness that in a hundred cases to one *causes and must cause* the wreck of the last means that is left us for ennobling our race.

At this time the child has no counterpoise that can be opposed to the phenomena of the world and the one-sided charm of its impressions on the senses; and so its conceptions, both through their one-sidedness and through their vividness, maintain a decided preponderance over the impressions of *experiences* and feelings *which lie at the base* of the moral and spiritual improvement of our race. Henceforth an infinite and infinitely living field is opened up for selfish and degraded passions. On the other hand, the way to that state of mind on which the powers of his intelligence and enlightenment rest is lost; that path to the narrow gate of morality is blocked up; the whole sensuousness of his nature must take a direction separating the *path of reason* from that of *love,* and the *improvement of the mind* from the *impulse towards faith in God*—a way that more or less makes selfishness the one driving wheel of all his actions, and thereby determines the result of his culture to his own destruction.

It is incomprehensible that mankind does not recognize this *universal source of ruin.* It is incomprehensible that it is not the one *universal aim of their Art* to stop it, and to *subordinate* the education of our race to *principles* which do not destroy the *work of God,* the feelings of love, gratitude, and trust already developed in infancy, but which must at this dangerous time tend specially to care for those *means of uniting our moral and spiritual improvement* implanted in our nature by God Himself, and of bringing education and instruction into harmony on the one side with those *laws of the physical mechanism* according to which our God raises us from vague sense-impressions to clear ideas; and on the other with *those feelings of my inner nature* through the gradual development of which my mind rises to recognize and venerate the *moral law.*

It is incomprehensible that mankind *does not begin to bring out a perfect gradation of methods of developing the mind and feelings,* the essential purpose of which should be to use the advantages of instruction and its mechanism for the preservation of moral perfection; to prevent the selfishness of the reason by preserving the purity of the heart from error and one-sidedness; and, above all, to *subordinate* my sense-impressions to my convictions, my eagerness to my benevolence, and my benevolence to my righteous will.

The causes which make this subordination necessary, lie deep in my nature. As my physical powers *increase,* their *preponderance,* by virtue of the laws of my development, *must vanish,* that is they must be *subordinated* to a higher law. But every step of my development must be completed before it can be subordinated to a higher purpose. This subordination of that which is already complete to that which is to be completed, requires above all pure *holding fast* to the *beginning-points* of all knowledge, and the most exact continuity in gradual progress from these beginning-points to the final *completion.* The primary law of this continuity is this: the first instruction of the child should never be the business of the *head* or of the *reason;* it should always be the business of the senses, of the *heart,* of the *mother.*

The second law, that follows it, is this: human education goes on slowly from exercise of the senses to exercise of the judgment. It is for a long time the business of the *heart,* before it is the business of the *reason.* It is for a long time the business of the *woman* before it begins to be the business of the *man.* . . .

PESTALOZZI'S AIMS

Friend! I go further now and ask myself: What have I done to work against the evils that affected me throughout my life, from a religious point of view? Friend! If by my efforts I have in any way succeeded in preparing the road to the goal at which I have been aiming, that is to take human education out of the hands of blind Nature, to free it from the destructive influence of her sensual side and the power of the routine of her miserable teaching, and to put it into the hands of the noblest powers of our nature, the soul of which is faith and love; if I can only in some slight degree succeed in making the Art of education begin in the sanctuary of home, more than it now does, and to put new life into the religious instinct of our race from this tender side; if I should only have partly succeeded in bringing nearer to my contemporaries the withered rootstock of mental and spiritual education, and an Art of education in harmony with the noblest powers of heart and mind: if I have done this, my life will be blessed, and I shall see my greatest hopes fulfilled. . . .

VII

VIEWS AND EXPERIENCES

THE PERIOD of eminently successful educational activity at Burgdorf was brought to a close in 1804 when the recently reestablished cantonal government requisitioned the castle in which Pestalozzi's school was located and offered him as a substitute the use of some monastery buildings at Münchenbuchsee. The conditions here not proving satisfactory, Pestalozzi removed to Yverdon where with two of his disciples he established a school in the castle, the use of which had been tendered him by the citizens. Here during an interval of unwonted quiet and freedom from care, he devoted himself to a review of his educational activities, both practical and theoretical, which he entitled *Views and Experiences*. The work is in the form of a series of letters and though incomplete, is an unusually clear and connected account both of his educational views and of the circumstances under which they developed.

Views and Experiences

Seyffarth, 9, 203–250

A GLANCE AT MY EDUCATIONAL AIMS AND EXPERIMENTS

General Survey. From my childhood up it lay in the peculiarity of my character and of my home training to be benevolent and kindly and to have unlimited confidence in those about me. This tendency led me early into association with the suffering and the unsuccessful and through this into a thousand experiences which awakened in me the profoundest sympathy for them and for the nature and the multiplicity of their sorrows, and convinced me at the same time of the urgent necessity of seeking some effective means of eradicating the multifarious causes of the evils which they endured.

Living at a time and in a fatherland where the better educated youth were generally inspired to search freely for the causes of the evils of the time and to a living zeal for the remedying of these, I also devoted myself to the task (as did all the pupils of a Bodmer and a Breitinger, and as it behooved the contemporaries of an Iselin, a Blaarer, a Tschiffeli, a Jetzeler, a Fellenberg, of several Eschers, Hirzel, Tscharner, Wattenwyle, Grafenriede and of so many other noble men to do) of seeking out the sources of the evil which kept the people of our fatherland so far below what they could be and ought to be.

As everywhere, we found it in the conflux of a great many dissimilar but powerfully cooperating and deeply and variously active circumstances, relationships, views, arrangements and customs through which the individual man in the country was forced to sink into a condition of powerlessness and helplessness which made it impossible for him to be that which he, as a man under the protection of God and as a citizen possessing legal rights, should and ought to be.

I soon convinced myself that there lie in the nature of every man powers and means originally sufficient to create for him a satisfactory existence and that the obstacles which oppose the development of these human talents and abilities can be overcome. As this conviction matured in me, the task of actually overcoming these obstacles appeared to me as a duty, the fulfillment of which would make men generally better fitted for the serious business of life.

The greater the evils, the removal of which I desired, and the more vividly I felt that the physical and mental powers of the people for the removal of these were unnaturally restricted and almost entirely paralyzed—the more clearly did experience show me that the deeds of charity with which people tried to combat these evils, instead of removing them, only stimulated their growth and that the only effective means of overcoming them consisted in developing and vitalizing the power originally innate in every man of satisfying his needs and of meeting the demands of the business, the duties and relationships of life and thus making him independent both for times of peace and of extremity.

The more clearly I saw this the more I felt impelled to strive toward this end. For this I wished to accomplish something definite and without delay. I did not wish merely to set up a better method of caring for the poor but rather to make it possible for even the poorest in the land to develop his physical, mental and moral capacities by himself and by means of the necessary circumstances in which he lived, in part, personally, and, in part, as a member of a family and as a citizen, and through this development to lay a firm foundation for a peaceful and contented life.

The first step in this direction to which the combined energy of my conviction and of my heart impelled me, was that of introducing a considerable number of beggar children and of waifs into my house in order to rescue them from their degraded condition and to restore them again to manhood and to their higher destiny and through this to demonstrate the correctness of my views both to myself and to those about me.

On all sides simple, thorough, and far-reaching, my undertaking sought all its means for accomplishing this end preferably in those situations where the need of self-help and the lack of external means make the development of great power urgently necessary and force the individual to the efforts requisite for the development of this power.

But this development was to be not only forced but also humane, and, to this end, in its inception and in the means employed, it was to be permeated by the spirit of a well-ordered home or, rather, it was to partake of the character of the influence of a parent upon the education of the child.

Whatever this influence might be able to afford the child under the most advantageous circumstances, just that my institution was to afford him, and the means by which the former brought to the child what it did, were to be, practically, the same as those which I employed in my institution to the same end.

From youth up I had a sort of reverence for the home influence upon the education of children and also a decided preference for agriculture as the most common, most comprehensive and purest foundation of folk education and at the same time I abhorred—perhaps too one-sidedly —the feudal system which had deprived the peasant class of the dignity which human nature claims for it and which sharply contrasted with the powerful urge toward moral, intellectual, domestic and financial independence fostered by the free constitution of the fatherland. It stood out in sharp contrast also to a sense of respectability common among the peasant class which had its roots in the condition above mentioned. . . .

The means to be employed for the salvation of the fatherland seemed clearly discernible and practicable. I believed that I could neutralize the most oppressive consequences of the evils of the feudal system and of the factory system through renewed effort for the education of the people to increased productivity in home and farm work and to a greater degree of self-respect. At the same time I hoped to counterbalance this by a clearer apprehension of noble, purely humane and unselfish political principles. Meanwhile I did not wish merely to dream that help could be afforded in this way nor to deceive and lead myself astray by setting up something that might merely have the appearance of public well-being. I wished to take up the work in a manner that would accord with the nature of man and with the nature of the circumstances in which man needs assistance. My institution was to be based upon a foundation of facts through the demonstration of which I could train myself for work and convince those about me of the truth of my views as to my undertaking and thus interest them in my work. I wished to include in its activities an adequate training for agriculture, for domestic management, and for the industries. But, however much I felt that my institution required this, I was no less convinced that every vocational training which did not provide the individual with a commensurate cultivation of the head and the heart would not only be inadequate but would be unworthy and would degrade him to the status of one slavishly trained merely for making a living.

So agriculture, domestic training and industry could not be my entire aim. Education to manhood was my aim; and for the attainment of this I considered agriculture, domestic economy and industry merely as a means. The more I saw the fatherland overwhelmed by the increased opportunities for making money afforded by the industrial revolution the less I sought for this money or for the refinement of the branches of industry in themselves, but rather for both as a means of securing what was especially needed, the maintenance and the stimulation of the development (*Belebung*) of pure manliness in all the people of the country. For this exalted end, more important than any considerations of money-making or manual skill, I desired to have the moral, intellectual and physical capacities of the individual well cared for in their common centre and to know at the outset that this more general education was assured rather than merely the particular parts of human education and other merely subordinate aims.

In addition to assuring the pupil of physical maintenance through training him for a reliable bread-winning occupation, I worked toward this end of a general education, relying entirely upon the head and the heart of the child, convinced that in this way his entire existence would be raised to a higher plane, and, in consequence, his bread-winning capacities better established. In this way, all efforts to make a living would necessarily lose their merely animal significance and thus become more truly valuable.

When, however, taking this view of things, I saw the great majority of mankind educated merely to skill in certain occupations and forced by their circumstances and their education itself, without ever having their real humanity developed, to waste their lives in a soulless and heartless round of manual labor, this condition of affairs could not other than call forth in me a heartfelt sympathy for the repressed and suffering masses. And when I then further saw that everywhere the men who held offices in church and state and were thus in a position not only to lighten the burden of intellectually, morally and economically oppressed mankind but also to put an end to the evils resulting from their unnaturally repressed and restricted condition, when I saw them, like conspirators, united to declare that the beastly plight of the people and, indeed, all repression of mankind in soul and body, was good, and, when I saw them with all the weight of their official prestige do everything possible to perpetuate this condition of things, my sympathy changed to a passionate revolt in my inmost soul against the injustice and against the devilish power to which the unfortunate majority of our race must submit and through which they have been degraded to a condition more like that of the ox before the plow than the condition of man in the dignity and power of that inner nobility to which he has been destined, not only by the nature of his inborn capacities, but also by the existence of means of advancement which through the providence of God have been prepared for his use for thousands of years.

I had friends, I loved, I had a fatherland, I had rights, but I did not wish to live. It seemed to me as if no man whose heart beat for friendship, love, and fatherland, for human nature and for its dignity should wish to live amidst conditions in which he himself as well as his children, his friends, his relatives, his fellow citizens, deprived of all means of attaining true humanity, were condemned to lead a merely animal existence.

Taking this view of the matter and in the mood of love and trust which this view naturally inspires, I dimly foresaw, even as a youth, the means which must be employed in order fully to satisfy the needs of human nature in all that pertains to the education of our race. I was much encouraged when, upon earnestly facing the problem, it occurred to me that the much misunderstood, but nevertheless essential and powerful, means to this end lay in the natural surroundings and relationships of the poor and the wretched. It awakened in me the highest hopes that I was convinced that necessity and want bring forth, in the case of the child of the poor, what every teacher needs for his pupil, namely, attention, effort and ability to overcome. Anything which is called forth in the child by natural means exercises a truer and more profound influence than what is called forth by artificial means. . . .

The less I was able to deceive myself as to the true condition of the poor, the more I endeavored out of a sense of duty to afford them assistance suited to the demands of their position and circumstances. Aware from personal experience of the magnitude of the powers which Nature herself develops in the poor, I eagerly sought in these powers a means of relieving their need. I was impelled to find work and training for work for the poor children whom I had taken into my house. But it was not merely this that

I sought. I wished during their work and by means of it both to warm their hearts and to develop their minds. I wished not merely to instruct them, but that their own life and activity should instruct them and should through self-instruction, elevate them to a sense of the inner dignity and worth of their natures. I wished above all to provide for the culture of the heart, as the noblest part of their being, as the central point in which were united the highest and purest of all the endowments both of the mind and of practical capacity. I was convinced that only in this way was it possible to integrate all the various means of educating humanity and especially the poor, and, even in the midst of innumerable incitements to wildness and dissipation, to maintain that loving, protective and considerate treatment which alone is capable of realizing the possibilities of vocational and intellectual education.

To this extent I was in a fortunate position for the prosecution of my enterprise. My life was fitted, as were the lives of few others, by a background of vivid experiences to establish the unalterable conviction that everything possible which one might attempt for ensuring the economic independence and even the intellectual development of the poor would fail to afford a truly human education if it were not carried on in a manner that had a soothing and elevating influence on the heart.

What was individual in my ability to achieve this end consisted in the vigor with which my heart impelled me to seek love wherever I could find it, to act in a friendly and pleasing manner wherever such action was possible, to endure, to control myself and to protect. I knew no greater happiness than the grateful look and the confiding grasp of the hand. It was to me a source of joy to deserve confidence and gratitude even where I could not hope to win them. It was in this frame of mind that my circumstances brought me into closer touch with the poor in the country. I sought out the poor, I gladly spent my time with them and this confirmed my views as to my central aim so as to render my confidence in myself and my purpose invincible in proportion as great and decisive experiences daily convinced me that a sincere and unselfish love for the poor would accomplish even through weaker efforts for their education a great good which stood in no relation to the apparent means employed. Just as, where the opposite feelings are dominant, the most magnificent institutions for folk education, folk welfare and the care of the poor are built upon sand and have to seek the cause of their failure in the nature of their foundation. I must have had experiences which showed decisively that love is powerful even in the weak and that without love the strength of the mighty is dissipated. But my undertaking demanded more than this conviction. In order to found an institution which would meet the demands of my aims in their entirety, much was needed which I notably lacked just in proportion as the interest in, and desire for such an institution was a feature of my personality.

I lacked essentially a calm, cold-blooded view of the object toward which I struggled as well as a calm observation and treatment of the men and things through which I might attain my aim. In general I lacked the strength both to avoid those influences which might injure my budding aims and to await without impatience the growth of every part of my institution to maturity. . . . The institution required an organization which would ensure the attainment of its aims. This was lacking and necessarily so. I should have had at hand for every subject for which I was not trained, educated men. I did not have them. The location should have been chosen with care, and equipped for my undertaking. It was not . . . Even my devotion to my institution and the self-forgetfulness and self-sacrifice with which I dedicated myself to my aims laid serious obstacles in my path. I sacrificed myself where I should not have done so, I hesitated where I should have stood firm, I hoped where I should have feared, I trusted where I should have demanded a reckoning, I gave thanks where I should have brought to account, I laid upon my shoulders what I was not able to bear, in order to take the burden from others who should and could have borne it.

Unable to attain what I sought I only exhausted myself, plunged myself into domestic confusion and into a condition of helplessness and powerlessness which caused me indescribable suffering and which lasted half a century.

During this long period the yearning of my heart, to live for the poor and the wretched, ceased not, yet, surrounded by all sorts of obstacles and the most oppressive restrictions, the flame of this desire availed nothing.—The men about me saw only my increasing helplessness. Meanwhile they had no perception of the cause of this helplessness, still less did they offer me any kind of assistance in the one thing for which I was capable. . . .

THIRD LETTER [1]

Friend! In order to determine from experience what good education essentially is, you must observe man in all

[1] The first and second letters are omitted.

his efforts and activities and in all his sufferings. You must look about you where he, in all his efforts and activities and in all his sufferings, stands among his fellow men as one who is what he ought to be. When you do that and you hear it said, "That is a man who is what all men should be," in reference to one who is still living and exercises an influence upon the intellect and feelings of those who testify of him, then you may doubt the truth of the statement. But if you hear this said at his grave in sight of his coffin and of the children, the aged and the poor who weep for him, then hold this testimony as sacred.

Indeed here thousands may say: "We have never heard this said. No such testimony is ever given among men. Even where there is one who deserves it, it is never given." But I say, "Does no one ever die for whom the poor weep? Of whom the aged man who knew him, the widow who loved him, the orphan who venerated him and the neighbor who lived in intimate relations with him, says, 'Is there still such a man as he on earth? Would that all men were such as he.'"

You say: "The best and noblest often sink into their graves misunderstood and even reviled." Friend! Even when they are misunderstood and vilified those who know them more intimately weep for them and exclaim: "Would that those who did not know them and who slander them were what these misunderstood and vilified men were!" But let us pass these by. He who sinks into the grave slandered and abused is not the man to whom I would direct your attention. . . .

There are men who live and die who, without being so unfortunate as these, without slander and abuse, bear with them into the grave this testimony, "They were men such as we all should be." But do not look for them in the midst of the tumult of life. Seek for them in the peace and quiet of the humble home.

Not that men even in the flurry of life and occupying even the most exalted positions might not carry this testimony with them into the grave, but the bustle and stir of their surroundings disturbs [sic] the simplicity of their lives and the correctness of statements as to their relations to their fellow men in death as in life. Of course even in the homes of the poor the men of whom the people can bear this testimony are rare. But if you seek him there and possess a nature which will fit you to recognize him you will surely find him and will hear the testimony: "That was a man, that was a woman who was what all should be," in many more instances than you could imagine. Believe it then, it will not lead you astray. It will show you what you should do for your child if you wish that people should bear the same testimony of him after his death. But do not stop at this. Turn to the oldest and most reliable among those who have testified and ask him just what it was in the deceased which led the people to do him honor. He will undoubtedly reply, "He was a man upon whose wisdom, sympathy and sense of duty one could confidently rely." He will say, "This man in his judgments, in the advice he gave, and in all his undertakings, gave evidence of possessing a sound and trained understanding, a firm, powerful and benevolent heart, capable of every exaltation and of every effort, and a skill and steadfastness in action which ensured him success in every instance."

In regard to the one-sided man who manifests excellence

in only one department of human activity you will not hear it said, "He was a man such as we all should be." No, you will not hear this said of the man who, even though possessing extraordinary acuteness of mind, capitulates to the selfishness of his feeble-heart and lives without love or sympathy in the midst of his suffering fellowmen. Neighbors and acquaintances will never hear this said of the man who, though possessing the heart of an angel and capable of extraordinary self-sacrifice in sharing the sorrows of others, nevertheless errs in the means employed and is unskillful in manifesting his sympathy and helpfulness even to those whom he most loves. . . . Simple, honest human nature will make this statement only of the man in whom insight, strength and will for the good are united in equal measure; of the man who in all the points of contact and relationships of his external life, in all his dealings and activities displays fully and in due proportion that disposition and that capacity proper to mankind.

He whose best and noblest actions lack this completeness and harmony but who, nevertheless, is distinguished by his goodness above his neighbors and fellow villagers and leads a noteworthy and serviceable but one-sided life; at his grave the simple peasant will only say, "He had a good head and a good heart and he did well in his calling"; but he will not say, "All men should be as he was."

Whenever you actually hear this great testimony do not be satisfied merely with knowing who this man was. Enquire further how he came to be what he was. A hundred to one the aged man who spent his youth with him will reply: "Father and Mother, domestic surroundings and relationships aroused and nourished in him in many ways the capacity for and the inclination toward the goodness which distinguished him throughout his life. Society and his fatherland extended for him in many ways the field for the exercise of this goodness, and a pious faith in God and eternity raised him, in this exercise, above considerations of himself, of his home, his fatherland, of the world and all its selfishness, to a capacity for lofty self-sacrifice for truth and justice which won for him the hearts of all men." And if you heard him himself—if at his grave he could, in the humility which he loved and which was fundamental in his life, if he could thank God for his guidance as in life he thanked him for it, he would say that the essential feature of the training which he enjoyed consisted in this that he was not given a training of the head or of the heart or for a vocation exclusively but that he was at one and the same time thoroughly and harmoniously trained in all three. He would relate the circumstances through which a nobler will was developed in him and by which both for his mind and his hand every effort toward the attainment of the goal of his life was facilitated. He would tell you how his efforts reacted upon him because of the care bestowed upon the harmonious provision for the needs of his entire being, how his activity and effort were reflected in this harmony, how it inspired him to gratitude and to love toward God and man, how this gratitude and love increased the happiness of his life, how it made it easier for him every day to do what he should and, through the doing of this, to become what he ought.

FOURTH LETTER

The testimony of simple human nature at the grave of a good and noble man. "He was such a man as all should be," is based upon a consciousness of the fact that "Man is an independent whole and is of value in himself and in his community only in so far as in all his relationships he is what he should be." And when the more profound student of human nature says: "Man must in his training be considered and treated as an independent being, unless one would make him worse by his training than he ever would have been without the interference of any kind of artificial means of education, he must be so educated that all the essential elements and motives of his nature are harmoniously stimulated and in all that he is, and for everything that he does, these must be made effective at the same time and in common, when he says this, he means, essentially, nothing different from what simple common sense causes every good man to feel who beside the grave of a man of noble character, says, "He was a man such as we all should be." Every more profound student of human nature must ultimately come to the conclusion that the education of man has no other goal than the harmonious development of the powers and capacities, the co-existence of which have made him through the grace of God a well-organized whole. He must always at the conclusion of his investigations come to see that only then is a man what he ought to be when his parents, his children, his neighbors, his fellow-citizens and especially the poor and the oppressed bear witness: "He was a man on whose head and heart and vocational skill one could rely. He showed in all his judgments a sound understanding, in everything that he advised and in everything that he undertook he revealed a strong character capable of any effort and any endurance, and in any occurrence that appealed to his heart he manifested an incorruptible integrity, an all-embracing benevolence and a noble spirit capable of any wise sacrifice; and since thus the results of his practiced understanding, of his lofty spirit and of his trained practical capacity everywhere interpenetrated each other, it followed of necessity that everything that he did proved adequate to the demands of himself and of others, and through this he came to be recognized as a man, such as all should be, and, as such, treasured and beloved."

The man who will himself bring his child up to this goal of perfection, whether he be a profound student of human nature or a simple peasant, the man who wishes to make of his child what, according to his nature, he can and ought to become must ask himself above all: "What is there in the child himself and, secondly, in his surroundings and connections which nature uses for the education of all men and by which she affords a secure foundation and a safe guide for the art of education." The answer to the second question depends, however, upon the answer to the first. . . . Taking both together it is evident that capacity for feeling, thinking and doing and stimulation to thought from without constitutes all that Nature employs for educating man according to his nature. This is what Nature indicates and provides to this end as a secure foundation and a reliable guide for the art of education. Everything that man achieves in power and mankind in the progressive development of our race is derived from feeling, from activity, and from the stimulation to both of these. The life of the individual man and of his race considered in general is nothing other than a continuous expression and a mutual interchange of feeling, of action, and of stimulation to both. If one considers this feeling, action, and stimulation as a whole he sees that the sacred, the good, the educative, and that which in all this leads man to harmonious perfection, proceeds from one central point and this regulates, directs, stimulates and restricts the above in accordance with a higher conception of the inner sanctity of our nature. And now it is incontrovertible that of all *feelings* it is the feeling of love in which alone the essence of that higher conception finds its purest expression and which is that central point by which all other feeling must be regulated, directed, stimulated, and restricted in order to remain in harmony with it.

Again, similarly, of all *activities,* it is the activity of the intellect which, since it develops in our nature along with love, expresses this higher conception, that activity by which all other human activity must be guided, regulated, stimulated, and restrained if it is to achieve a harmonious and complete development of our capacities and thereby really ennoble them. Love and that intellectual activity which develops along with love are plainly the fixed beginning-point from which the development of all our powers proceeds and must proceed.

It is altogether impossible to make of the child what he should be in order to live among his fellow-men as a contented, high-minded human being, fully meeting the demands of his situation in life unless careful attention is given to the development within him of love and all-round intellectual activity, and to bringing these into harmony with each other. Man, as a being capable of raising himself above the enticements of his sensual nature and under obligation to do this, finds the means of meeting the demands of his destiny in nothing other than in this harmony between his love and his activity. His equipment, also, for rising to the demands of his destiny and his duty, is as thorough and complete as the tendency to this is human, inasmuch as it has its origin in love, depends upon activity, and is associated with freedom.

FIFTH LETTER

Just as there exists in our nature a capacity for love and activity adequate to the realization of our destiny so there exists without, in our surroundings and relationships various stimuli and incitements of this capacity for the ennoblement of ourselves through love and activity. And just as all that is holy and elevating and stimulating in all our feeling and action issues from the feeling of love and from the higher activity of our intellectual nature, so what is holy, exalting and educative in the incitements of the child by his surroundings to love and activity proceeds from his parents and from his relations to them as from a central point. The influence of all other features of the child's surroundings which affect his training for love and activity is heightened and ennobled by their connection with this centre. While the inner source of everything that is to make the child thrive in body and soul is in the child itself, its outer source is in the care of the parents. These two sources have a thousand points of contact and are essentially interdependent and inseparable.

Hence, where the care of real parents is lacking, every-thing possible must be done to provide it artificially. When-ever father and mother are deficient whether morally, in-tellectually or physically—the father and mother spirit must be provided in his education, if the child is to be educated to true humanity. If this is not done the unfortunate or-phaned child, in spite of all schooling and of all food and clothing that may be provided, will lack the first essential of a truly human education. But where this is present, where the child enjoys the care which the spirit of father-hood and mother provides, the impression which the child receives is one of love which impels him to reciprocal love, to gratitude and trust and to all inner and outer activity of the higher capacities of our nature. Thus this impression is fitted to supply, at least up to a certain point, the physical and moral lack of real parents so far as education to hu-manity is concerned. Through this sacred father and mother care the entire environment of the child becomes a means of satisfying his intellectual and emotional needs even though the physical presence of the actual parents is lack-ing. Every bite of bread which the child eats, if it is given him by a loving mother, becomes something quite different, as regards his training to love and activity, from what it would be if he found it on the street or received it from the hand of a stranger. The stocking which she knits before his eyes becomes for his training to love and activity something far different from the stocking which he buys at the market or obtains otherwise without knowing whence. The mother-love which provides enjoyment for the child is an impulse to an unfailing higher inner life which stimulates the child to love, to gratitude, to trustfulness, and rouses to activity all the higher capacities of his nature.

This explains why the life of the home must be considered the only God-given external basis of truly human education. It alone affords all the incentives and motives and even the need and the compulsion by which Nature as divine vicegerent develops and establishes in us the capacities of our race. The bond which unites the members of the home circle is essentially the bond of love and it is the God-given means of awakening love. In its purity this life is the highest, the most exalted that can be thought or dreamed of for the education of our race. It is unconditionally true: where love and the ability to love are found in the home circle there one can confidently predict that the education it affords almost never fails. The child must be good, he can scarcely be otherwise. The result of his education follows almost as a matter of necessity. On the other hand one can assert with something approaching definiteness that in all cases where the child is lacking in good will, vigor and activity the fault lies in the fact that his love and his lovability failed to find in his home life that nourishment and direction which it needed. Wherever the child finds these it will certainly develop vigor and goodness of character. It cannot fail to do this. Since the child is lovingly cared for daily and hourly in this sanctuary it is constantly incited to love in return. As it gradually comes to take a hand in caring for itself it at the same time begins to aid father and mother in the satisfaction of their needs and desires. . . . Thus, in the life of the home, labor and love, obedience and effort, gratitude and industry combine, each strengthening and invigorating the other. The man who loves, spares no effort on behalf of the object of his love, and the love, which labors, leads through the inner and outer activity which inspires it to a corresponding intellectual vigor and to an effective employment of mind and heart in the achievement of everything which love and insight may set up as a goal to be attained.

Of course the certainty of the effectiveness of a system of home education suited to the needs of human nature presupposes a father and mother who themselves exemplify this love and the higher activities which spring from it. . . . It presupposes parents to whom the world in deed and in truth is as nothing compared with their child. It presupposes men, who, whether they sit on a throne or dwell in the cottages of the poor, pay no heed to the claims of the world so far as these conflict with those of their children. Men, who, conscious of their inner strength, feel in their hearts the truth of the statement: "Could I gain the whole world and yet should my child suffer harm what recompense for this should I possess?" . . .

Such, O lover of thy fellow-man, whether thou sittest on a throne or dwellest in an humble cottage, who desirest the elevation of thy race and seekest to do what is necessary to aid them, such are the fathers and mothers who will and can be for their children what they should be. In vain is thy heart set on the ennoblement of thy people if thou dost not seek here its foundation for thou shalt find it nowhere else. The book of human nature is revealed to the child only in the parental feelings of the father and mother. The sacred expression of the purer and nobler feelings and powers which have been inscribed in this book by the flaming pencil of the Creator is the definite, unchanging expression of the feelings peculiar to this sense of parenthood and of the faculties awakened and cultivated by this sense.

It is the joy of the parents' life to see the delight which sparkles in the eye of their child when his heart overflows with love. It is a joy and a source of inner content to see the peace which hovers on his brow and on his lips when the child rests in their arms in perfect trust, the meaning of which he does not understand. They are happy when they recognize in the eye of the child its gratitude and absolute dependence while it shows in a thousand ways that no one in the world arouses in him the feelings which Father and Mother arouse. The most sacred of their feelings are aroused when they see the innocence of the loving child, as if moved by some inner force, gladly doing or refraining from doing what he sees in the eyes of his parents what they would have him do or not do. It uplifts them within to recognize the happiness of love and gratitude, the peacefulness of trust and the innocence of the powers developed in dependence and obedience as something sacred in the child, with the life and growth of which they are more concerned than with the life and growth of his body. Inspired by these feelings, the heart of both the father and the mother cannot but impel them to be for their child all that they ought to be in order to cherish and cultivate in him those sacred impulses and tendencies engendered by parental love and care.

Surrounded by the impurities of the world these divine impulses sprout forth from his innermost being; like the most delicate plant, they need warmth, nourishment, pro-

tection and careful attention and find all this in the strength
and love of the father and mother. And if you succeed,
and through the watchful, protective and assisting activity
of your fatherly and motherly loyalty there develops in
your child a divine impulse which ripens to full expression
in strength and love and he stands before you loving and
working as a reflection of yourself, and as your child feels,
desires and acts as you would have him, . . . Father and
Mother what power is yours? It is a divine power to cause
to develop in thy child everything that is noble and good
in human nature through the sacred virtue of thy care and
watchfulness. It is a divine power to direct with wisdom
and to restrain with firmness from the beginning that
sensuality which is so necessary to what is sacred in our
development and which so easily becomes overmastering
and destructive. You can achieve the greatest object which
the most highly developed educational art can aim at, you
can with assured success prevent the child's deviations from
the path of truth and innocence without losing his love and
without undermining his childlike and confiding frankness.
The more firmly the might of your affection opposes what
is false, and destructive in his tendencies, the more you win
his confidence and attach him to yourself by the purest
impulses of his heart. Through your action you call up at
the outset of the conflict between his sensual nature and
his better self, moments in which the conviction that the
severity of your opposition is but another aspect of your
gentleness and goodness, arouses within him a determina-
tion to oppose with the same severity everything which you
oppose, and to second all your efforts for the ennoblement
of his character.

And now withdrawn from this vision of a purified and ennobled fatherhood and motherhood . . . withdrawn from the contemplation of the elevating influence of the father and mother which leads the child unerringly and directly along the narrow path to a higher life, victoriously overcoming all obstacles, I find myself in the midst of a world in which I seek far and wide in vain for such parents. The world as it actually is, given over to sensuality, and selfishness oppresses so heavily the divine element in human nature, the impulse toward truth and love. Even the father and the mother belong to this world. There is in them, in your surroundings . . . in the severity and in the pomp and display of the forms of civic organization and in the ever-increasing refinement of these, so much mind-and-heart-confusing, love-destroying, enervating and degrading opposition and violent hostility against that higher nature on which the attainment of the lofty aim of child education depends that one must not wonder at the ever-increasing distance which separates mankind from the path which leads to this end. One should wonder rather that man has not only not submitted to these forces but has maintained the struggle toward a higher life and in the midst of his errors and his weakness, continues to recognize love and benevolent activity as the only means by which his nature may be truly exalted.

This effort and this recognition of the only true foundations for the education of our race can and will never disappear in human nature. Rather than this, our nature itself will disappear. The best and noblest men will always in all circumstances recognize the genuineness of their parental feelings and impulses as the foundations of whatever is noble and lofty in their characters. And whatever stands the test of experience in the education of our race, whatever proves adequate and sufficient, will always and invariably be found to be related to this divine sense of fatherhood and motherhood; this will hold true even where this feeling has been dwarfed through the deleterious influence of a degenerate social environment and however much, deprived of all attractiveness and charm, it may have been exposed to humiliation and ridicule. Nevertheless, the harmful influence of the deplorable spirit of our times, so lacking in love, wisdom and energy, increases the difficulty of the task of disseminating among men the beneficence of this sense of fatherhood and motherhood. It restricts, confuses, and misdirects even the individual private efforts toward this end, which are made in the homes of our best and noblest citizens.

WHY SCHOOLS ARE A NECESSITY.

Seyffarth, 9, 289–292

The life of the home, the tender care of the mother, the strength of the father, the atmosphere of love and sympathy, the interaction of each with all, the education by work, the totality of these good influences acting upon each in a group bound together by the ties of nature, all this constitutes a framework to which one might easily attach everything essential to a good education.

But this does not mean that this is actually done. Thousands who find their welfare and happiness in the life of the home circle make very little use of it in the education of their children. The reasons for this are various. The chief one is that the effectiveness of home education does not keep pace with social development. On the contrary the more a race advances socially the more difficult it is for individuals to satisfy through the influence of home life the educational needs which have multiplied so much in response to the demands of public education. Moreover, the more zealously men endeavor to satisfy the occasional and arbitrary demands of social education the greater the danger they incur of overlooking the demands of nature, of failing to recognize the importance of the means which the home affords to this end. They become incapable of pursuing a natural system of education in proportion as they acquire skill in one that is showy and artificial. But aside from these errors incident to our increasing social refinement, men, while recognizing the advantages of home life, must always feel that these are scattered and unrelated and are difficult to collect and organize and use. The results of individual experiments and the means of acquiring skill and of extending one's knowledge are lacking even in the best-ordered households and the urgent demands of domestic and civil life deprive many parents of the time requisite for the thorough instruction of their children.

In order to compensate for these almost unavoidable limitations of home education schools were established. Their aim was to make good the deficiencies of home education and to fill out the gap between the limited possibilities of home life and the steadily increasing demands of society and to this end to bring within the reach of all the culture possessions of the race.

In view of their essential aim it is the duty of the schools to secure for the pupil the advantages of home life in educating him to be a man and a citizen and to increase these and make them more generally available. They should strengthen and develop those means of education, reflection, love and vocational training, which are already in the home and should combine new with the older means of accomplishing its end.

In intimate harmony with home life they (the schools) should afford a continuation, an expansion and completion of the powers and capacities which naturally develop in the home. Where they actually accomplish this they deserve the respect of the people and the gratitude and confidence of every good father and mother, even where in the interests of liberal or vocational education their work seems to be one-sided.

One must not, however, make the mistake of considering the result of this one-sidedness as a complete and adequate education of our race; on the contrary one must seek in the power that has already been developed, genuine though one-sided, a means for developing those capacities in which the child has been deficient. Every faculty, even though one-sided, if it be truly and completely developed can also be used. There lies in human nature an inner connection between everything that is good. The complete development of a single one of its capacities demands the development of all the others and facilitates this development in all of them. Notwithstanding their limitations the schools of a people may exercise a decisive influence on their welfare.

Should the school, however, abandon its unnatural and accidental role of promoting the development of only some of the talents and capacities and take up that of satisfying the essential needs of human nature as does a well-ordered home life its influence in aiding human nature to attain the goal of its existence would be assured.

VIII

PESTALOZZI'S ADDRESS TO HIS HOUSE ON THE OCCASION OF HIS SEVENTY-SECOND BIRTHDAY, JANUARY 12, 1818

THE ADDRESSES which Pestalozzi was accustomed to deliver before his school at Yverdon on New Year's day and on other festive occasions are valuable not only for the occasional, illuminating presentations of his doctrines which they contain but also as revelations of his character. In them the warmly affectionate, sensitive, child-like soul of Pestalozzi reflects in its alternations of joy and sadness the varying fortunes of his educational activities. The address from which the following selections are taken includes one of the most helpful of Pestalozzi's expositions of his aims and of his views as to how these may be achieved. It was delivered on the occasion of his birthday in 1818. Dissension among his teachers had resulted in the withdrawal of a considerable number. The sadness occasioned by this defection was at this time relieved somewhat by the prospect of a considerable increase of income to be derived from the recently arranged publication of his complete works. In the course of the address Pestalozzi announced the assignment of a large proportion of this prospective income to various enterprises for promoting the cause of education.

*Pestalozzi's Address to His House on the Occasion of His
Seventy-Second Birthday, January 12, 1818*

Seyffarth, 10, 531–571

As the tree grows so does man. Already before the child
is born there are to be found in it the germs of the capacities
which will unfold throughout its later life. Just as all the
separate parts of the tree cooperate, under the influence of
the invisible vital force of its physical structure, in the
production of its fruit, so all the fundamental powers of the
human being cooperate under the influence of an unseen
force in the human organism in the production of a man,
a being made in the image of God. . . .

Man! Examine yourself and seek to find out in what
ways you attain harmony within yourself and how you
come to be at war with yourself and with your fellow-men.
See in what ways you can come to be a friend of faith, of
love, of truth, and justice, and, on the other hand, how you
may come to be an enemy of all these. Examine yourself
closely. Take a broad view of the whole process of the
development of a man. See, he grows, he is trained, he is
educated. He grows by his own power. He grows by virtue
of a force that lies within himself. His character has been
moulded by accident by the accidental in his circumstances
and his relationships. He has been educated by the art and
the will of man. The growth of a man and of his powers
is God's affair. It takes place in accordance with eternal
unchanging divine laws. The involuntary education of man
is accidental and dependent upon the varying circumstances
in which he finds himself. The deliberate education of a
man is moral. It is a result of the freedom of the human

will in so far as it exercises an influence upon the development of his powers and capacities.

Through the growth of his talents and capacities man is
a creation of the divine laws which lie within himself.

Through his involuntary education he is a product of the
influence which his accidental circumstances and relationships have had upon the freedom and purity of his growth.

Through his deliberate education he is a product of the
influence which the moral will of man has upon the freedom and purity of his powers.

The law of man's growth is in itself divine and eternal.
The influence of his involuntary education is earthly and
sensual. Uncertain and accidental in itself, is the influence
of his deliberate education.

The involuntary and voluntary education of man is to be
considered as an aid to the inner impulse toward development.

The influence of the environment can be brought into
harmony with the natural growth of human powers. Deliberate education should be brought into harmony with it.
But both may be brought into conflict with it.

The mist of illusion in which we have been led astray
in matters of popular education and of the care of the poor
must be dissipated in the light of the true art of education
and of the care of the poor.

But in what does this art consist and what is it? I answer
it is the art of the gardener under whose protective care a
thousand trees grow and flourish. Notice that he contributes nothing to their growth in itself. Their growth depends
essentially upon themselves.

He plants and waters and God gives the increase. It is

not the gardener who opens the roots of the tree that they may draw in sustenance from the soil. It is not he that separates the heart of the tree from the wood and the wood from the bark and continues this division from the roots to the outermost twigs, . . . Of all this he does nothing. He only waters the dry earth . . . and he drains away the standing water that it may not become stagnant. He only takes care that no external force should injure either the roots, the trunk or the branches. So the educator. It is not he who endows man with capacity of any sort; he only sees to it that no external force should hinder or disturb natural course of development of any capacity. . . .

But the educator who wishes to bring the art of education to bear upon the development of human capacities should have a thorough knowledge of the human organism. . . . He knows that just as the true means of the education of the people must consist in the harmony of the human art in the development of our powers with the eternal laws according to which these powers themselves unfold, so these means must be sought in all that strengthens and purifies the moral and religious bond which unites all our powers. . . .

Friends of humanity! From my youth up the aim of my life has been to provide a happier future for the poor of the land through simplifying the means of education and instruction and basing them on a firmer foundation. It has never been my good fortune, however, to be able to exert a direct influence upon the education of the poor. I sought in a round about way through the establishment of a boarding institution to find the way to my goal. But this did not have financially the success which I sought. It did, however, afford me an opportunity of investigating more minutely and comprehensively the means which are necessary for the culture and education of our race and in this I was assisted by friends, by whom the ideas of elementary education which developed in my mind and by which our efforts were especially characterized, were tested and worked over. It is quite certain, however, that the idea of elementary education is nothing else than a living expression of the above-mentioned double point of view, and, from my youth up, my endeavor has been based upon an obscure feeling of this need, and not merely as it generally lies in human nature but as it expresses itself especially as a need of our time; for we must not conceal from ourselves that in days when the will, the abilities and the knowledge of men are nourished and built up by a simpler and more vigorous life there is less urgent need of a search for a higher grade of art in the means of education of our race than in times when the mis-education of our race is fostered by an artificial refinement, to such a degree as it is in ours.

Hence, living in surroundings and circumstances very advantageous for the investigation of the principles of elementary education and forcibly restricted to the beginning points of this education it could not well happen otherwise than that the fundamental ideas and principles should gradually attain in me to remarkable clearness.

Just as the beginning of the united activity of my house was to a high degree lively and vigorous and seemed to justify expectation of prompt and many-sided results, so the later years of our efforts, deprived of the liveliness and exaltation of the first years, did not seem to justify the hopes which we had aroused at the beginning. It could not be otherwise. We were not adequate to the huge task which we had imposed on ourselves and owing to the limitations of human nature we could not be. We should not have imposed it on ourselves and yet it is good that we did so. We encountered indeed a thousand difficulties which we had not anticipated. But firmly convinced of the attainability of our aims, we tried every means that seemed to lead to the goal and in this way the dead stop to which we were brought served to increase our knowledge of our aim, and this was for us truly important. I soon came to recognize the identity of what was essential in the education of all classes and became convinced also that it is not the development of knowledge in any particular field, nor the development of any particular kind of skill but the development of the powers of human nature itself which is the essence of the education of children of all classes from the richest to the poorest.

I early voiced the need, in *Leonard and Gertrude,* for greater attention to the controlling center of all human capacities, the will, and sought to bring the living-room of the home to public attention as the center for the inauguration and the prosecution of all educational measures. In my later years and especially since the founding of my boarding establishment I have, in cooperation with my friends, endeavored to organize the several means of developing the individual powers and capacities in a psychological sequence corresponding to the course through which nature herself develops these powers. The cultivation of these several powers, respectively, in accordance with the laws of nature has seemed to my house almost ever since its origin to be the problem the solution of which should be considered the task of the pedagogy of our time. The association of friends who since the beginning of the century have constituted my house have been actively engaged throughout this whole period in the investigation of this problem. We all feel that we are still infinitely far from the goal which we have tried to reach. Great personalities also have participated in our great and human undertaking. But in what great undertaking is it otherwise?

If the thought of one man becomes the thoughts of hundreds, so from one thought develop a hundred thoughts no one of which is any longer the thought of the first from whom the thought emanated. That is God's law. . . .

I was not entirely unfortunate in my feeble effort notwithstanding the shocks it had to endure from the events of the time. I believe I may express the belief that the century whose beginning witnessed the inauguration of our pedagogical investigations will still at its close witness the uninterrupted continuation of our efforts by men who are indebted for their views and equipment to the united activities of our house.

I believe in the uninterrupted continuation of my efforts and am even quite undisturbed in the face of all the circumstances which retarded their results, confused the course of their development and even raised doubts in me as to the correctness of my views. The sorrows of my life have really been great but my career is drawing to a cheerful close.

Even that which I for so long considered to be the chief misfortune of my life, namely, that I had to become an old man before I could lay hand to the work of educating the masses and the poor—has now ceased to be such. I am now firmly convinced that if I had actually engaged earlier in life in the education of the poor, I should not have found myself as prepared as one should be who makes plans and provides means which will actually have upon national culture, upon the condition of the people in general, and especially, upon the enjoyment of the blessings of life by the poor, that influence which they should have.

. . . The mature idea of elementary education demands directly that scientific knowledge be a product of the cultivated mind and not that the cultivated mind should be a product of knowledge. There can be no true art of education, there can be no true art of training men to humanity without reverent observance of the divine plan in the laws of development which lie within man himself. All measures and rules which lack this foundation are nothing else than the daily wages on the air-castle of a sham culture which only confuses and disturbs the powers of human nature and which is in its essence adapted to afford nourishment and scope to the selfishness of an unbrotherly and unchristian life.

Hence, I thank God that throughout my life I have not been able to actually take a hand in the education of the poor until I have been able to attain a grasp of these loftier views and have arrived at the conviction that the art of education must essentially, and in all its parts, be raised to a science which is a product of the profoundest knowledge of human nature and is built upon it. I am indeed far from having attained a knowledge of this science. I have only an imperfect conception of it. But this conception has acquired a vitality that fills my whole soul as if it were already a complete reality. This is the case not only with

me. The conditions of the time have made it a world necessity. The world will recognize it and will note with loving
care the token which I today lay upon the altar of humanity
in this solemn hour, in which I also call upon you to work
with me in what I believe myself still able to accomplish
in inaugurating and directing the education of the people
and in basing it upon more natural and pedagogically better
organized principles. This work I am ready and am determined to maintain and to defend beyond the grave. . . .

The only sure foundation on which we can have folk
education, national culture and aid of the poor is the heart
of the father and the mother which through the innocence,
truth, power and purity of its love kindles in the children a
faith in love. Through this faith all the bodily and mental
powers of the children unite in obedience to love and in
active obedience.

It is in the sanctuary of the living-room that the harmonious development of human capacities takes place, guided
and assured by nature herself, and it is on this fact that the
art of education must be based if national education is to be
a real benefit to the people and to bring the externals of
human knowledge, capacity, and impulse into harmony
with our inner divine nature.

If the statement is true *inventis facile est addere* [1] it is
infinitely truer that it is easy to add to the inner, eternal
Good of our human nature the external Good which human
art can give to our race, but to reverse that and to endeavor
to educe the eternal and divine Good of our human nature
from the poverty of our human art alone, is the cause of the

[1] It is easy to make additions to what has already been discovered.

profound confusion which characterizes the artificial procedure of our time. The living-room of the common people,
I do not say of the rabble—the rabble has no living-room—
I say the home circle of the people is at the same time the
point in which everything that is divine in the educational
influences of human nature is centered. Here, where, as
God has decreed, stores of influence lie ready at hand, it is
easy for human art to add the tribute of its service; but
where the art, paying no heed to the home circle, casts its
tribute into the filth of the outer world or lays it as an
idolatrous sacrifice upon the altar of selfishness and seeks
to educate children without the aid of father and mother
and, I might say, without God and the home circle, there
the art amounts to little because it supplements nothing,
and the little becomes nothing, and when it becomes nothing, it confirms the truth of the saying, "Whoever has nothing, from him shall be taken even that which he hath." And
we must not conceal from ourselves the fact that the spirit
of our times has brought it about that we are all in the air
so far as the home circle and its beneficent influence are
concerned.

The great and almost unsurmountable evil of our times
is this that parents have almost entirely lost confidence in
their ability to educate their children. This great lack of
faith in themselves, on the part of fathers and mothers, is
the one general source of the ineffectiveness of our system
of education.

Hence in order to promote the education of the people
it is above all necessary to revive in parents the conviction
that they possess the ability to promote the education of
their children. Fathers and mothers must be brought once

again to realize how superior, in all that relates to the education of their children, they are to those, who, as teachers and assistants, participate in a function which, by divine ordinance, is primarily that of the parents. In this connection it is highly desirable that that feeling should be revived among the people which led the ancients to provide for a child who had been so unfortunate as to lose its natural educators, its father and mother, the ablest educator obtainable. It is still more to be desired that the joy, which parental influence upon the education of children affords to those who exert it should be more generally recognized. This is necessary if the sacred desire for this enjoyment is ever to be revived in the hearts of the parents. It is urgently necessary that the parents of our time should be brought to a realization of the inner barren emptiness into which every human soul must sink which has lost that power which the parent naturally exerts upon the education of his or her children. The modern world needs to realize that loss of the influence of the father and the mother in the education of humanity means not only the loss of that civic stability and contentment which characterized our forefathers but also the loss of the sacred foundation of a noble, pure, Christian home life.

We must not conceal from ourselves the fact that it is in the relation of the inner to the outer, it is through the preponderance of the inner over the outer, that we are enabled to advance toward a genuine national folk culture and to combat the evils of the present.

I shall not touch upon the measures which should be taken, by the Church and the State, in order to foster a better spirit in our home life; I shall discuss only the means toward this and which might emanate from an enlightened and philanthropic pedagogy.

The friends of education should work together for the production of a book for the people, adapted to teach fathers and mothers the extent of the influence they might exert upon the education of their children. This should be a book for mothers and for the family circle. The book must be capable of arousing us out of the state of indifference toward education in which the views, the passions and the habits of our time have placed us. It requires perhaps herculean labor, it requires the cooperation of the higher humanity of our time, the cooperation of the most distinguished powers of charm, of insight and artistry of our race for the gradual production of such a mother-and-family-circle-book as will serve with certainty to revive the faith of individual fathers and mothers of all classes in their ability to carry on the training and the education of their children. It should vividly impress fathers and mothers with the attractiveness of their task. It should simply, and with convincing charm, reveal the many situations and circumstances which home life affords the parents for leading the children to exercises of their senses, to uplifting emotional experiences, to edifying surveys of their surroundings, to gradual, psychologically organized, direct knowledge of objects of nature and of art, leading to a scientific knowledge of these objects. Finally it should make clear to fathers and mothers the simplicity of the means by which the children's powers of reasoning may be cultivated in successive stages, and how they may be trained to the various kinds of skill which all art . . . and vocational training presupposes. In a word it should, with the greatest simplicity and art, contribute to the development in the family circle, and by practicable means, of the child's knowledge, will, and practical ability in a manner suited to his nature.

It is impossible, however, to attain this end, and the writing of the book will be impracticable, just as long as the attempt is not supported by a persistent and continuous investigation of ways and means by which human nature itself develops every individual capacity of our race according to its own laws and then brings these individual capacities, according to higher laws, into harmony with the totality of their powers.

The efforts of the friends of humanity to prepare the way for a real national folk culture must begin with a carefully maintained investigation of the ways of nature herself in the development of our race, and must be founded on this.

To this end, it is no less important that the instruction in each individual science should harmonize with the fundamental powers of human nature whose development the science presupposes, and that the exercises and other means through which the science is learned should be in harmony with the procedure through which the powers were themselves developed. At the same time the investigation into the course of nature in the learning of each science must show what parts of the subjects can be correctly and satisfactorily learned through direct experience, what parts through the exercise of the memory or of the imagination, and, further, what parts of the subject may be used, on the one hand, as a means of exercising and training the faculties and, on the other, as mere materials for the learning of the science. And this must be done before the mental and physical powers which the science presupposes are really there. Just as clay, stone, lime, and sand are often brought to a location long before the actual building is begun.

It is also essential to this end to establish a really universal system of education so that the efforts to use speech, number, and form as the elements of thought may be carried on energetically and carefully, and that, in their application, they may be brought into harmony with the elementary exercises through which the genial powers of faith and love as well as the elementary physical powers of our race are naturally developed.

This plain need for the inauguration of a truly national culture implies the necessity of combining number and form, as the spiritual means of cultivating the art powers, with an elementary training of the physical powers which depends primarily on the elementary training of the eye and hand, and leads to the introduction of a general gymnastic of the physical powers.

It is impossible, however, that these measures and views should have a real influence upon the culture of the people unless the knowledge and skill of the present becomes general. Hence it is absolutely necessary that the training of the home circle and that of the school should each influence the other. Only in this way can this knowledge and skill become the common possession of the people and be prized and used as a benefit both to the home and to the country. Experimental schools must also be established in which the means for the elementary mental and physical education of the people are made familiar to the children so that every child leaving the school would be in a position to impart to its brothers and sisters the knowledge and skill acquired. In this way parents would be prepared to conduct not only the mental but the physical training of their children. A review of the conditions which must be met in order to inaugurate a true psychological system of national and folk education convinces me that it is quite practicable. But the evils under which the country suffers are great and we must not think that it is an easy matter to remedy them. I repeat it again, the evils of our lack of culture and of the moral, mental, and physical backwardness of our people have their roots in the opinions, desires and habits characteristic of our time. I should like to say again that they seem to be an outgrowth of a well-established world order, and are to be removed only through the application of better principles and measures of folk education, and of the care of the poor. I am quite aware that it will require both time and courage to bring about the needed transformation in the system of popular education and I am also quite aware of the fact that what I can contribute is only a trifle compared to the great sacrifices which the philanthropy and the enlightenment of our race are to make to the needs of the time. But just this need of our time awakens in me the hope that thousands of the friends of humanity will contribute their part toward the attainment of this end. For my part, I have not permitted myself to be prevented from making every endeavor to contribute my mite toward this end. The seven conditions under which alone I believe the establishment of a general system of national and folk education to be possible have been in great measure especial objects of investigation and of effort throughout my entire life and my present circumstances are well adapted to ensure the continuation of the investigation and application of some of these both during my life and after.

The principal need of our time, a handbook for mothers, especially in regard to the means for educating their children which lie ready at hand, has been for a long time a favorite idea of mine and I shall not fail to work toward its realization throughout my life. And just as I do not feel myself entirely powerless in my old age, so far as this first condition for the establishment of a national system of education is concerned, so I find myself here in Yverdon favorably situated for work upon the other six. . . .

The gymnastic training preparatory to industry requires a city location. One would be, for this work, at a great disadvantage in the country or in a village. . . .

The aim of every influential educational institution should be to exert, through its principles, its methods and results, an influence not merely upon particular individuals but upon human nature in all relationships and circumstances so that the willing, knowing and doing of the good and the needful should be disseminated among all classes. In all classes men should be led to be God-fearing, intelligent, philanthropic and useful in the home and to the state. The incentives and the means to all this are never to be found in the social classes and relationships of men; they are to be found only in the higher and nobler nature of man and in everything which inspires man with enthusiasm for this.

On the other hand man in his social relationships is tempted on all sides to forgetfulness of God, to self-seeking, to heartlessness, thoughtlessness and laziness, in brief to all the vices and follies of life. Everywhere education through training and the cultivation of intelligence should enable man to withstand the temptations of his sensual nature, should make habitual in him the practice of the contrary virtues, and should accustom him to the moral, intellectual and physical effort and achievement without which a higher and nobler human life is unthinkable.

Now it is evident that stern necessity impels the poor to reflection, to activity, to self-mastery, to effort, to moderation, to patience, and to the acquisition of many kinds of skill, to a degree which does not hold true of the rich. Education must exercise art to bring the wealthy and aristocratic to attainments which the child of the poor or middle class acquires without any assistance. The distinction between the education of the rich and the poor lies essentially in this, that greater insight must be used in leading the former to effort and activity while on the other hand toil and struggle must lead the latter to thought and reflection, to knowledge and insight. . . .

In the family circle is to be found everything that is highest and most sacred for the people and for the poor. It is the benign influence of the family circle which alone can help the people and it is this aid which is today most urgently needed. From it issue the truth, the power and the blessing of the culture of the people. . . .

Elementary training in its essence is nothing other than a return to the true art of education, to the simplicity of home training. This art is truly an exalted one. The means it employs, the true means of elementary training, are not individual contributions of knowledge or of art which are like water which one brings in buckets and pours upon the dry soil. This poured-out water soon disappears. The soil dries out again and remains dry until again a good man brings and pours out another bucket and moistens it again. No, no, the true means of education are like living springs, which, when once opened, continue forever to moisten the soil which they bless. The results of true elementary training are not merely temporary, they are not the vain enjoyment of individual gifts of knowledge and of art. They are the genuine vitalization of the powers of human nature, out of which issue the knowledge and the ability of our race like living water from the unfathomable rock. In their essence they are one with the spirit and the beneficent influence of life of the home circle, and the beneficent consequences, which their union with this life must have, are incalculable.

Hence, if I ask myself: What can and what should I do in order to establish a genuinely national and popular system of education? I must answer: Elevate the elementary means of mental and art training in their entirety and in all their branches to a simplicity which will make them applicable in the home of the common man.

It is indisputable that in the living-room of every household are united the fundamental means for the true education of mankind.

From the moral and religious point of view the tie which binds father, mother and children is at the same time the source of all views and feelings which lead man through faith and love to all that is exalted and eternal, and prepares him in the earthly enjoyment of the love of father and mother for sonship with God, and, through the obedience of faith in father and mother, exalts him to the obedience of faith in God. . . .

As regards the intellect, all investigation and all reflection of the members of the household issues from the love and gratitude and trust which binds them together.

From the physical point of view it is the same. All activity of the members of the household, every activity of the father and the mother in the care of the children as well as all efforts of the children in obedience toward their parents and in cooperation in the service of all, have their origin in faith and love. . . .

If, therefore, I proceed directly toward my goal and endeavor through my subscription to establish and promote that which I am convinced is most essential for laying the foundations for a true national and popular education, I must seek to promote through it everything which may contribute to establish, and promote and insure the welfare of the home circle.

I assign, therefore, the sum of 50,000 French livres from the proceeds of the sale of my works as an irreducible fund, the annual interest of which is to be applied,—

1. To the persistent investigation and testing of principles and procedures by which popular instruction and training may be simplified and adapted for use in the home circle.

2. For the training of men and women teachers for this work.

3. For the erection of one or more experimental schools in which children may be taught and trained in accordance with the prescriptions above mentioned.

4. For the continued working over of a book for mothers and

for the home circle with the end in view of making home training and instruction more and more complete and effective. . . .

The history of Europe shows that in our part of the
world marked progress has been made at different times
toward maturity of knowledge; but in order properly to estimate from the historical point of view the great value of the
right kind of home life and its tremendous influence on
the education of the people, cast a glance at the Reformation period, the third jubilee of which we have just cele-
brated, and see how at that time every household, moved
by the spirit of the times, found in the family union a
common centre for the improvement of the condition of
the home circle and a basis for a grade of moral, intellectual
and domestic culture, which promoted the general welfare
of the people to such a degree that those who did not share
in it have been lagging in the rear even to this day.

IX

THE LETTERS TO GREAVES

One of the clearest expositions of his educational views
is presented by Pestalozzi in a series of letters sent in
1818 and 1819 to his friend, James Pierrepont Greaves,
a philanthropic Englishman, who, during his stay at
Yverdon, had given instruction in English to the children of Pestalozzi's school for the poor at Clindy.
Translated into English by a German named Worms,
they were published in England in 1827. Two years
later they were reprinted in the *American Journal of
Education*.

The Letters to Greaves

LETTER III

October 7, 1818.

My dear Greaves,

Every mother who is aware of the importance of her
task, will, I presume, be ready to devote to it all her zeal.
She will think it indispensable to attain a clear view of the
end for which she is to educate her children.

I have pointed out this end in my last letter. But much
remains to be said on the means to be employed in the first
stage of education.

A child is a being endowed with all the faculties of hu-

146

man nature, but none of them developed: *a bud not yet opened*. When the bud uncloses, every one of the leaves unfolds, not one remains behind. Such must be the process of education.

No faculty in human nature but must be treated with the same attention; for their co-agency alone can ensure their success.

But how shall the mother learn to distinguish and to direct each faculty, before it appears in a state of development sufficient to give a token of its own existence?

Not indeed from books, but from actual observation.

I would ask every mother who has observed her child with no other end but merely to watch over its safety, whether she has not remarked, even in the first era of life, the progressive advancement of the faculties?

The first exertions of the child, attended with some pain, have yet enough of pleasure to induce a repetition gradually increasing in frequency and power; and when their first efforts, blind efforts as it were, are once over, the little hand begins to play its more perfect part. From the first movement of this hand, from the first grasp which avails itself of a plaything, how infinite is the series of actions of which it will be the instrument! not only employing itself in everything connected with the habits and comforts of life, but astonishing the world, perhaps, with some masterpiece of art, or seizing ere they escape the fleeting inspirations of genius and handing them down to the admiration of posterity.

The first exertion of this little hand then opens an immense field to a faculty which now begins to manifest itself.

In the next place the attention of the child is now visibly excited and fixed by a great variety of external impressions: the eye and the ear are attracted wherever a lively color, or a rousing animating sound, may strike them, and they turn, as if to inquire the cause of that sudden impression. Very soon the features of the child, and its redoubled attention, will betray the pleasure with which the senses are affected by the brilliant colors of a flower, or the pleasing sounds of music. Apparently the first traces are now making of that mental activity which will hereafter employ itself in the numberless observations and combinations of events, or in the search of their hidden causes, and which will be accessible to all the pleasing or painful sensations which life in its various shapes may excite.

Every mother will recollect the delight of her feelings on the first tokens of her infant's consciousness and rationality; indeed maternal love knows not a higher joy than that arising from those interesting indications. Trifling to another, to her they are of infinite value. To her they reveal an eventful futurity; they tell her the important story, that a spiritual being, dearer to her than life, is opening as it were the eye of intelligence and saying in its silent, but tender and expressive language, "I am born for immortality."

But the last and highest joy, the triumph of maternal love, remains yet to be spoken of. It is the look of the child to the eye of the mother—that look so full of love, so full *of heart,* which speaks most emphatically of its elevation in the scale of being. It is now a subject for the best gift bestowed on human nature. The voice of conscience will speak within its breast; religion will assist its trembling steps and raise its eye to Heaven. With these convictions the heart of the mother expands with delight and solicitude: she again hails in her offspring not merely the citizen of earth: "Thou art born," she cries, "for immortality and an immortality of happiness: such is the promise of thy heaven-derived faculties; such shall be the consummation of thy Heavenly Father's love."

These then are the first traces of human nature unfolding in the infantine state. The philosopher may take them as facts constituting an object of study: he may use them as the basis of a system; but they are originally designed for the mother—they are a hint from above, intended at once as her blessing and encouragement:

> For all her sorrows, all her cares,
> An over-payment of delight!

LETTER XII

December 8, 1818.

My dear Greaves,

We have seen that the animal instinct is always intent on instantaneous gratification, without ever adverting to the comfort or interest of others.

As long as no other faculty is awake, this instinct and its exclusive dominion over the child cannot properly be considered as faulty; there is not yet any consciousness in it: if it be selfish in appearance, it is not wilfully so; and the Creator himself seems to have ordained that it should be so strong, and indeed exclusively prevailing, while consciousness and other faculties could not yet contribute to secure even the first conditions of animal life—self-preservation.

But if after the first indication of a higher principle this instinct be still allowed to act unchecked and uncontrolled as before, then it will commence to be at war with conscience, and every step in which it is indulged will carry the child farther in selfishness, at the expense of his better and more amiable nature.

I wish this to be clearly understood; and I shall perhaps better succeed in explaining the rules which I conceive to flow from it for the use of the mother, than in dwelling longer on the abstract position. In the first place, let the mother adhere steadfastly to the good old rule, to be regular in her attention to the infant; to pursue as much as possible the same course; never to neglect the wants of her child when they are real, and never to indulge them when they are imaginary, or because they are expressed with importunity. The earlier and the more constant her adherence to this practice, the greater and the more lasting will be the real benefit for her child.[1]

The expediency and the advantages of such a plan will soon be perceived, if it is constantly practised. The first advantage will be on the part of the mother. She will be sup-

[1] "It seems plain to me that the principle of all virtue and excellence lies in a power of denying ourselves the satisfaction of our own desires, where reason does not authorize them. This power is to be got and improved by custom, made easy and familiar by an *early practice*. If, therefore, I might be heard, I would advise that, contrary to the ordinary way, children should be used to submit their desires and go without their longings *even from their early cradles*. If the world commonly does otherwise, I cannot help that. I am saying what I think should be done, which, if it were already in fashion, I should not need to trouble the world with a discourse on this subject." LOCKE *Education,* pp. 25–26, Cambridge University Press, 1902.

ject to fewer interruptions; she will be less tempted to give way to ill-humor; though her patience may be tried, yet her temper will not be ruffled: she will upon all occasions derive real satisfaction from her intercourse with her child; and her duties will not more often remind her than her enjoyments that she is a mother.

But the advantage will be still greater on the part of the child.

Every mother will be able to speak from experience either to the benefit which her children derived from such a treatment or to the unfavorable consequences of a contrary proceeding. In the first instance their wants will have been few and easily satisfied; and there is not a more infallible criterion of perfect good health. But if on the contrary that rule has been neglected; if from a wish to avoid anything like severity a mother has been tempted to give way to unlimited indulgence, it will but too soon appear that her treatment, however well-meant, has been injudicious. It will be a source of constant uneasiness to her without giving satisfaction to her child; she will have sacrificed her own rest without securing the happiness of her child.

Let the mothers who have been unfortunate enough to fall into this mistake tell whether they have not had frequent occasion to repent of their ill-timed indulgence, unless they had the still greater misfortune of substituting in its place the other extreme—a habit of indolence and cold neglect. And let the children who were brought up in early youth under an excess of indulgence, tell whether they have not been suffering under the consequences; whether hurrying on from excitement to excitement, they have ever felt that health and tranquillity, that evenness of spirits, which is the first requisite to rational enjoyment and to lasting happiness.

Let them tell whether such a system is apt to give a relish for the innocent sports, for the never-to-be-forgotten feats of boyhood; whether it imparts energy to withstand the temptation, or to share in the noble enthusiasm of youth; whether it ensures firmness and success to the exertions of manhood.

We are not all born to be philosophers; but we aspire all to a sound state both of mind and body, and of this the leading feature is—*to desire little, and to be satisfied with even less.*

LETTER XIV

December 17, 1818.

MY DEAR GREAVES,

From the reasons stated in my last letter, I think it right to assume that maternal love is the most powerful agent, and that affection is the primitive motive in early education.

In the first exercise of her authority, the mother will therefore do well to be cautious that every step may be justified by her conscience and by experience; she will do well to think of her responsibility, and of the important consequences of her measures for the future welfare of her child; she will find that the only correct view of the nature of her own authority is to look upon it as a duty rather than as a prerogative, and never to consider it as absolute.

If the infant remains quiet, if it is not impatient or troublesome, it will do so *for the sake of the mother.*

I would wish every mother to pay attention to the difference between a course of action adopted in compliance with *the authority* and a conduct pursued *for the sake of another*.

The first proceeds from reasoning, the second flows from affection. The first may be abandoned, when the immediate cause may have ceased to exist; the latter will be permanent, as it did not depend upon circumstances or accidental considerations, but is founded in a moral and constant principle.

In the case now before us, if the infant does not disappoint the hope of the mother it will be a proof, first of affection, and secondly, of confidence.

Of affection—for the earliest and the most innocent wish to please is that of the infant to please the mother. If it be questioned whether that wish can at all exist in one so little advanced in development, I would again, as upon almost all occasions, appeal to the experience of mothers.

It is a proof also of confidence. Whenever an infant has been neglected, when the necessary attention has not been paid to its wants, and when, instead of the smile of kindness, it has been treated with the frown of severity, it will be difficult to restore it to that quiet and amiable disposition in which it will wait for the gratification of its desires without impatience, and enjoy it without greediness.

If affection and confidence have once gained ground in the heart, it will be the first duty of the mother to do everything in her power to encourage, to strengthen, and to elevate this principle.

She must encourage it, or the yet tender emotion will subside, and the strings which are no longer attuned to sympathy will cease to vibrate and sink into silence. But

153

affection has never yet been encouraged except by affection; and confidence has never been gained except by confidence; the tone of her own mind must raise that of her child's.

For she must be intent also upon strengthening that principle. Now there is one means only for strengthening any energy, and that means is practice. The same effort, constantly repeated, will become less and less difficult, and every power, mental or physical, will go through a certain exercise with more assurance and success, the more it grows familiar with it by custom. There cannot, therefore, be a safer course for the mother to pursue than to be careful that her proceedings may without interruption or dissonance be calculated to excite the affection and secure the confidence of her child. She must not give way to ill humor or tedium, not for one moment; for it is difficult to say how the child may be affected by the most trifling circumstance. It cannot examine the motives, nor can it anticipate the consequences, of an action: with little more than a general impression of the past it is entirely unconscious of the future; and thus the present bears upon the infant mind with the full weight of pain, or soothes it with the undiminished charm of pleasing emotions. If the mother consider this well, she may spare her child the feeling of much pain which, though not remembered as occasioned by special occurrences, may yet leave a cloud as it were upon the mind, and gradually weaken that feeling which it is her interest as well as her duty to keep awake.

But it is not enough for her to encourage and strengthen, —she must also elevate that same feeling.

She must not rest satisfied with the success which the benevolence of her own intentions, and perhaps the disposition and temper of her child, may have facilitated: she must recollect that education is not a uniform and mechanical process, but a work of gradual and progressive improvement. Her present success must not betray her into security or indolence; and the difficulties which she may chance to meet with must not dampen her zeal, or stop her endeavors. She must bear in mind the ultimate ends of education; she must always be ready to take her share in the work which as a mother she stands pledged to forward—the elevation of the moral nature of man.

LETTER XVI

December 31, 1818.

My dear Greaves,

If the mother has once accustomed herself to take the view to which I alluded in my last, of the affection and the confidence of her infant, all her duties will appear to her in a new light.

She will then look upon education, not as a task which to her is invariably connected with much labor and difficulty, but as a work of which the facility and in a great measure the success is dependent on herself. She will look upon her own efforts in behalf of her child not as a matter of indifference or of convenience, but as a most sacred and most weighty obligation. She will be convinced that education does not consist in a series of admonitions and corrections, of rewards and punishments, of injunctions and directions, strung together without unity of purpose or dignity of execution; but that it ought to present an unbroken chain of measures, originating in the same principle—in a knowledge of the constant laws of our nature;

practised in the same spirit—a spirit of benevolence and firmness; and leading to the same end—the elevation of man to the true dignity of a spiritual being.

But will the mother be able to spiritualize the unfolding faculties, the rising emotions of her infant? Will she be able to overcome those obstacles which the preponderance of the animal nature will throw in her way?

Not unless she has first lent her own heart to the influence of a higher principle; not unless the germs of a spiritual love and faith which she is to develop in her child have first gained ground in the better affections of her own being.

Here, then, it will be necessary for the mother to pause and examine herself, how far she may expect to succeed in inculcating that to which in her own practice she may have been a stranger more than she would wish to confess to herself. But let her be sincere, for once; and if the result of her examination be less favorable to her own expectations and less flattering to her self-love, let her resolution be the more sincere and vigorous to discard for the future all those minor predilections, to check all those wishes which might alienate her from her new task; and to give her whole heart to that which will promote her own final happiness and that of her child.

However difficult it may appear at first to resign, to dismiss the thought of some hopes, and to defer the accomplishment of others, still that struggle is for the very best cause, and if serious cannot be unsuccessful: for there is not an act of resignation, there is not a single fact in the moral world, however distinguished, to which maternal love could not furnish a parallel.

If the mother is but conscious of the sincerity of her own intentions, if she has raised the tone of her own mind and elevated the affections of her being above the sphere of subordinate and frivolous pursuits, she will soon be enabled to ascertain the efficacy of her influence on the child.

Her best and almost infallible criterion will be whether she really succeeds in accustoming her child to the practice of self-denial.

Of all the moral habits which may be formed by a judicious education, that of self-denial is the most difficult to acquire and the most beneficial when adopted.

I call it a habit; for though it rests upon a principle, yet it is only by engendering a habit that that principle gives evidence of its vitality. The practice of all other virtues, and more especially many of the actions which are admired and held out as examples, may be the result of a well-understood moral rule which had long been theoretically known before it was applied in a practical case; or again they may have flown from a momentary enthusiasm, which acts with irresistible power on a mind alive to noble sentiments. But a practice of self-denial, conscientiously and cheerfully pursued, can be the fruit only of a long and constant habit.

The greatest difficulty which the mother will find in her early attempts to form that habit in her infant does not rest with the importunity of the infant, but with her own weakness.

If she is not herself able to resign her own comfort and her own fond desires to her maternal love, she must not think of obtaining such a result in the infant for her own sake. It is impossible to inspire others with a moral feeling if she is not herself pervaded with it. To endear any virtue to another she must herself look upon her own duty with pleasure. If she has known Virtue only as the awe-inspiring Goddess—

> With gate and garb austere,
> And threatening brow severe,

she will never obtain that mastery over the heart which is not yielded up to authority but bestowed as the free gift of affection.

But if the mother has in the discipline of early years or in the experience of life herself gone through a school of self-denial; if she has nourished in her own heart the principle of active benevolence; if she knows resignation, not by name only but from practice; then her eloquence, her look of maternal love, her example, will be persuasive, and the infant will in a future day bless her memory and honor it by virtues.

LETTER XVII

January 7, 1819.

My dear Greaves,

I am anxious to elucidate some statements of a preceding letter, concerning the early practice of self-denial. Allow me for this purpose to resume the subject of my last; and if I shall appear to have dwelt too long on a favorite theme or to have recurred to it too often, may I hope that you will ascribe this circumstance at least not *solely* to the loquaciousness of old age, but also to my conviction of the vital importance of the subject.

The more I have seen of the mental and moral misery under which thousands of our fellow-creatures are suffering; the more frequently I have observed the wealth without content, the splendor without happiness, among the higher classes; the closer I have investigated into the first springs of those mighty convulsions which have shaken the world and made even our peaceful valleys ring with the shouts of war and with the wailing of despair; the more have I been confirmed in the view that the immediate causes of all this and of much misery that yet remains unmentioned have arisen from an undue superiority which the desires of the lower nature of man have assumed over the energies of the mind and the better affections of the heart.

And I cannot see any remedy placed within the reach of human power to check the further progress of this misery and the ulterior demoralization of our race, but the early influence of mothers, to break by firmness the increasing power of animal selfishness, and to overcome it by affection.

This is the end to which I would wish the practice of self-denial to contribute. For this reason I insist on the circumspection to be employed by mothers in controlling the cravings of infants.

For this reason I would again and again request the mother to be watchful in her care, to do all in her power and to do it with cheerfulness, that none of its real wants may rest unattended to. For it is not only her duty to do so in order to provide for the physical well-being of the child; but a neglect of this duty is to be still more anxiously avoided because it might cast a shadow on her own affection, and provoke, if not doubts, at least a feeling of uneasiness which might afterwards lead to them.

But for this same reason I would entreat a mother to be constantly on her guard against her own weakness; never to indulge the appetite of the child with what may be stimulating to further desire or what is at best superfluous; and never to encourage importunity.[1]

What I call weakness she may perhaps call affection.

But let her be persuaded that the character of true affection is far different. The affection for which she would plead is merely animal: it is a feeling for which she cannot account and which she cannot resist. It may become to her also the basis of a more elevated feeling of spiritualized maternal love. But to experience the latter she must have opened her own heart to the influence of spiritual views and principles. She must herself know how to bear and forbear, to resign and be humble. She must know a higher object of her wishes, a purer source of enjoyment than present gratification. She must weigh the experience of the past and ponder the duties of the future. Her own interest and her own desires must not interfere with more momentous obligations, or weaken her attachment and her zeal for the welfare of others. Her affections must not be centered in self; her wishes and her hopes must not be limited to the things of this world.

[1] "An infallible way of rendering a child unhappy, is to indulge it in all its demands. Its desires multiply by gratification, without ever resting satisfied: it is lucky for the indulging parents, if it demand not the moon for a plaything. You cannot give everything; and your refusal is more distressing than if you had stopped short at first. A child in pain is entitled to great indulgence; but beware of yielding to fancy; the more the child is indulged, the more headstrong it grows, and the more impatient of a disappointment." LORD KAMES, *Loose Hints on Education,* Vol. I, p. 54, J. Bell and J. Murray, 1781.

What is born of the flesh must perish. If such be her af-fection to her child, it will die away before she is able to do anything for its real interest. But if her affection is of a higher origin; if its efforts bear the stamp of a calm, a mild, and a conscientious spirit, it will enable her to conquer her own weakness, and to elevate by a judicious control the rising emotions of her infant.

To those who have not had an opportunity of observing it frequently, it is impossible to form an idea of the rapidity and eagerness with which the animal instinct grows, if left to itself without the salutary check of maternal influence. *But the means so frequently employed even by mothers to restrain its growth by the fear of punishment can tend only to make the evil worse.* The mere act of forbidding is a strong excitement to desire. Fear can never act as a moral restraint; it can act only as a stimulus to the physical appe-tite; it exasperates and alienates the mind.

This then is gained by severity.[1] Its consequences are no

---

[1] "I absolutely prohibit severity; which will render the child timid, and introduce a habit of dissimulation—the worst of habits. If such severity be exercised, so as to alienate the child's affections, there is an end to education; the parent, or keeper, is transformed into a cruel tyrant over a trembling slave. Beware, on the other hand, of betraying any uneasiness in refusing what a child calls for unreasonably: perceiving your uneasiness, it will renew its attempt, hoping to find you in better humor. Even infants, some at least, are capable of this artifice; therefore, if an infant explains by signs, what it ought to have, let it be grati-fied instantly, with a cheerful countenance. If it desire what it ought not to have, let the refusal be sedate, but firm. Regard not its crying: it will soon give over, if not listened to. The task is easier with a child, who understands what is said to it: say only with a firm tone, that it cannot have what it desires; but without showing any heat on the one hand, or concern on the other.

doubt as mischievous as those of indulgence. Against an excess of both I can only repeat the recommendation of *affection and firmness*.

From these two guiding principles the mother will derive the satisfaction to see that when her infant from an inability to understand her motives cannot yet respect her as a wise mother, it will for the kindness of her manner obey her as a loving mother.

LETTER XX

January 25, 1819.

MY DEAR GREAVES,

In describing the manner in which the immediate influence of the mother is gradually weakened, and the connection between her and the child loosened, we must not stop at the enumeration of those facts which I have detailed in my last.

It is not the mere physical growth, the acquirement of the full use of all the faculties of the body, which constitutes the independence of the child. The off-spring of the animal creation have indeed reached the highest point of their development when they are strong enough to subsist and provide for themselves. But it is far otherwise with the off-spring of man.

In the progress of time the child not only is daily exercising its physical faculties, but begins also to feel intellectually and morally independent.

From observation and memory there is only one step to

The child, believing that the thing is impossible, will cease to fret." *Loose Hints on Education,* Vol. I, p. 48, J. Bell and J. Murray, 1781.

reflection. Though imperfect, yet this operation is frequently found among the early exercises of the infant mind. The powerful stimulus of inquisitiveness prompts to exertions which if successful or encouraged by others will lead to a habit of thought.

If we inquire into the cause of the habit of thoughtlessness which is so frequently complained of, we shall find that there has been a want of judicious encouragement of the first attempts at thought.

Children are troublesome; their questions are of little consequence; they are constantly asking about what they do not understand; they must not have their will; they must learn to be silent.

This reasoning is frequently adopted, and, in consequence, means are found to deter children from the provoking practice of their inquisitiveness.

I am certainly of the opinion that they should not be indulged in a habit of asking idle questions. Many of their questions certainly betray nothing more than a childish curiosity. But it would be astonishing if it were otherwise; and the more judicious should be the answers which they receive.

You are acquainted with my opinion that as soon as the infant has reached a certain age, every object that surrounds him might be made instrumental to the excitement of thought. You are aware of the principles which I have laid down, and the exercises which I have pointed out to mothers. You have frequently expressed your astonishment at the success with which mothers who followed my plan, or who had formed a similar one of their own, were constantly employed in awakening in very young children the dormant faculties of thought. The keenness with which they followed what was laid before them, the regularity with which they went through their little exercises, has given you the conviction that upon a similar plan it would be easy not only for a mother to educate a few, but for a teacher also to manage a large number of very young children. But I have not now to do with the means which may be best appropriated to the purpose of developing thought. I merely want to point to the fact that thought will spring up in the infant mind; and that though neglected or even misdirected, yet a restless intellectual activity must sooner or later enable the child in more than one respect to grow *intellectually independent* of others.

But the most important step is that which concerns the affections of the heart.

The infant very soon commences to show by signs and by its whole conduct that it is pleased with some persons, and that it entertains a dislike, or rather that it is in fear of others.

In this respect habit and circumstances may do much; but I think it will be generally observed that an infant will be easily accustomed to the sight and the attentions of those whom it sees frequently and in friendly relation to the mother.

Impressions of this kind are not lost upon children. The friends of the mother soon become those of the infant. An atmosphere of kindness is the most kindred to its own nature. It is unconsciously accustomed to that atmosphere, and from the undisturbed smile and the clear and cheerful glance of the eye it is evident that it enjoys it.

The infant, then, learns to love those whom the mother

considers with affection. It learns to confide in those in whom the mother shows confidence.

Thus it will go on for some time. But the more the child observes, the more distinct are the impressions produced by the conduct of others.

It will therefore become possible even for a stranger, and one who is a stranger also to the mother, by a certain mode of conduct to gain the affection and the confidence of a child. To obtain them, the first requisite is constancy in the general conduct. It would appear scarcely credible, but it is strictly true, that children are not blind to, and that some children resent, the slightest deviation, for instance, from truth. In like manner, bad temper once indulged may go a great way to alienate the affection of the child, which can never be gained a second time by flatteries. This fact is certainly astonishing; and it may also be quoted as evidence for the statement that there is in the infant a pure sense of the true and the right, which struggles against the constant temptation arising from the weakness of human nature to falsehood and depravity.

The child, then, begins to judge for himself not of things only but also of men; he acquires an idea of character; he grows more and more *morally independent*.

LETTER XXI

February 4, 1819.

My dear Greaves,

If education is understood to be the work not of a certain course of exercises resumed at stated times but of a continual and benevolent superintendence; if the importance of development is acknowledged not only in favor of the memory and the intellect and a few abilities which lead to indispensable attainments, but in favor of all the faculties, whatever may be their names, or nature, or energy, which Providence has implanted; its province, thus enlarged, will yet be with less difficulty surveyed from one point of view, and will have more of a systematic and truly philosophical character, than an incoherent mass of exercises, arranged without unity of principle, and gone through without interest—which frequently, not very appropriately, receives the name of education.

We must bear in mind that the ultimate end of education is not perfection in the accomplishments of the school, but fitness for life; not the acquirement of habits of blind obedience and of prescribed diligence, but a preparation for independent action. We must bear in mind that whatever class of society a pupil may belong to, whatever calling he may be intended for, there are certain faculties in human nature common to all, which constitute the stock of the fundamental energies of man. We have no right to withhold from any one the opportunities of developing all his faculties. It may be judicious to treat some of them with marked attention, and to give up the idea of bringing others to high perfection. The diversity of talent and inclination, of plans and pursuits, is a sufficient proof for the necessity of such a distinction. But I repeat that we have no right to shut out the child from the development of those faculties also which we may not for the present conceive to be very essential for his future calling or station in life.

Who is not acquainted with the vicissitudes of human fortune which have frequently rendered an attainment valuable that was little esteemed before, or led to regret the want of application to an exercise that had been treated with contempt? Who has not at some time or other experienced the delight of being able to benefit others by his advice or assistance, under circumstances when but for his interference they must have been deprived of that benefit? And who, even if in practice he is a stranger to it, would not at least in theory acknowledge that the greatest satisfaction man can obtain is a consciousness that he is preeminently qualified to render himself useful?

But even if all this were not deserving of attention; if the sufficiency of ordinary acquirements for the great majority were vindicated on grounds perhaps of partial experience and of influence from well-known facts, I would still maintain that our systems of education have for the most part been laboring under this inconvenience, that they did not assign the due proportion to the different exercises proposed by them.

The only correct idea of this subject is to be derived from the examination of human nature with *all its faculties*. We do not find in the vegetable or the animal kingdom any species of objects gifted with certain qualities which are not in some stage of its existence called into play, and which do not contribute to the full development of the character of the species in the individual. Even in the mineral kingdom the wonders of Providence are incessantly manifested in the numberless combinations of crystallization; and thus even in the lowest department of created things, as far as we are acquainted with them, a constant law, the means employed by Supreme Intelligence, decides upon the formation, the shape, and the individual character of a mineral, according to its inherent properties. Although the circumstances under which a mineral may have been formed or a plant may have grown or an animal may have been brought up may influence and modify, yet they can never destroy that result which the combined agency of its natural energies or qualities will produce.

Thus education, instead of merely considering what is to be imparted to children, ought to consider first what they may be said already to possess, if not as a developed, at least as an involved faculty capable of development. Or if, instead of speaking thus in the abstract, we will but recollect that it is to the great Author of life that man owes the possession and is responsible for the use of his innate faculties, education should not only decide what is to be made of a child, but rather inquire, what is a child qualified for? what is his destiny, as a created and responsible being? what are his faculties as a rational and moral being? what are the means pointed out for their perfection and the end held out as the highest object of their efforts by the Almighty Father of all, both in the creation and in the page of revelation?

To these questions the answer must be simple and comprehensive. It must combine all mankind—it must be applicable to all, without distinction of zones or nations in which they may be born. It must acknowledge in the first place the rights of man, in the fullest sense of the word. It must proceed to show that these rights, far from being confined to those exterior advantages which have from time to time been secured by a successful struggle of the people, embrace a much higher privilege, the nature of which is not yet generally understood or appreciated. They embrace the rightful claims of all classes to a general diffusion of useful knowledge, a careful development of the intellect, and judicious attention to all the faculties of man, physical, intellectual, and moral.

It is in vain to talk of liberty, when man is unnerved, or his mind not stored with knowledge, or his judgment neglected; and above all, when he is left unconscious of his rights and his duties as a moral being.

LETTER XXII

February 10, 1819.

MY DEAR GREAVES,

If according to correct principles of education all the faculties of man are to be developed and all his slumbering energies called into play, the early attention of mothers must be directed to a subject which is generally considered to require neither much thought nor experience, and therefore is generally neglected. I mean the physical education of children.

Who has not a few general sentences at hand which he will be ready to quote, but perhaps not to practice, on the management of children? I am aware that much has been done away with that used to exercise the very worst influence on children. I am aware that the general management of them has become much more rational, and that their tasks and amusements have been much improved by a judicious attention to their wants and their faculties. But much still remains to be done; and we shall deserve little credit for a real wish to improve if we suffer ourselves to rest satisfied with the idea that all is not so bad as it might be or as it may have been.

The revival of gymnastics is in my opinion the most

important step that has been done in that direction. The great merit of the gymnastic art is not the facility with which certain exercises are performed or the qualification which they may give for certain exertions that require much energy and dexterity; though an attainment of that sort is by no means to be despised.

But the greatest advantage resulting from a practice of those exercises is the natural progress which is observed in the arrangement of them, beginning with those which while they are easy in themselves yet lead as a preparatory practice to others which are more complicated and more difficult. There is not perhaps any art in which it may be so clearly shown that energies which appear to be wanting are to be produced, as it were, or at least are to be developed by no other means than practice alone.

This might afford a most useful hint to all those who are engaged in teaching any object of instruction, and who meet with difficulties in bringing their pupils to that proficiency which they had expected. Let them recommence on a new plan, in which the exercises shall be differently arranged and the subjects brought forward in a manner that will admit of the natural progress from the easier to the more difficult. When talent is wanting altogether, I know that it cannot be imparted by any system of education. But I have been taught by experience to consider the cases in which talents of any kind are absolutely wanting but very few. And in most cases, I have had the satisfaction to find that a faculty which had been quite given over, instead of being developed had been rather obstructed in its agency by a variety of exercises which tend to perplex or to deter from further exertion.

And here I would attend to a prejudice which is common enough concerning the use of gymnastics: it is frequently said that they may be very good for those who are strong enough; but that those who are suffering from weakness of constitution would be altogether unequal to and even endangered by a practice of gymnastics.

Now I will venture to say that this rests merely upon a misunderstanding of the first principles of gymnastics: the exercises not only vary in proportion to the strength of individuals; but exercises may be and have been devised for those also who were decidedly suffering. And I have consulted the authority of the first physicians, who declare that in cases which had come under their personal observation individuals affected with pulmonary complaints, if these had not already proceeded too far, had been materially relieved and benefited by a constant practice of the few and simple exercises which the system in such cases proposes.

And for this very reason, that exercises may be devised for every age and for every degree of bodily strength, however reduced, I consider it to be essential that mothers should make themselves acquainted with the principles of gymnastics, in order that among the elementary and preparatory exercises they may be able to select those which according to circumstances will be most likely to suit and benefit their children.

I do not mean to say that mothers should strictly adhere to those exercises only which they may find pointed out in a work on gymnastics; they may of course vary them as they find desirable or advisable; but I would recommend a mother much rather to consult one who has some experience in the management of gymnastics *with children*, before she decides upon altering the course proposed, or adopting other exercises of which she is unable to calculate the exact degree of strength which they may require or the benefit that her children may derive from them.

If the physical advantage of gymnastics is great and un-controvertible, I would contend that the moral advantage resulting from them is as valuable. I would again appeal to your own observation. You have seen a number of schools in Germany and Switzerland of which gymnastics formed a leading feature; and I recollect that in our con-versations on the subject you made the remark, which exactly agrees with my own experience, that gymnastics, well conducted, essentially contributes not only to render children cheerful and healthy, which for moral education are two all-important points, but also to promote among them a certain spirit of union and brotherly feeling which is most gratifying to the observer: habits of industry, open-ness and frankness of character, personal courage, and a manly conduct in suffering pain, are also among the natural and constant consequences of an early and a con-tinued practice of exercises on the gymnastic system.

LETTER XXIII

February 18, 1827.

My dear Greaves,

Physical education ought by no means to be confined to those exercises which now receive the denomination of gymnastics. By means of them strength and dexterity will be acquired in the use of the limbs in general; but particu-lar exercises ought to be devised for the practice of all the senses.

This idea may at first appear a superfluous refinement, or an unnecessary encumbrance of free development. We have acquired the full use of our senses, to be sure, without any special instruction of that sort: but the question is not whether these exercises are indispensable, but whether under any circumstances they will not prove useful.

How many are there of us whose eye would without any assistance judge correctly of a distance, or of the proportion of the size of different objects? How many are there who distinguish and recognize the nice shades of colors, without comparing the one with the other; or whose ear will be alive to the slightest variation of sound? Those who are able to do this with some degree of perfection will be found to derive their facility either from a certain innate talent, or from constant and laborious practice. Now it is evident that there is a certain superiority in these attainments which natural talent gives without any exertion, and which instruction could never impart though attended by the most diligent application. But if practice cannot do everything, at least it can do much; and the earlier it is begun, the easier and the more perfect must be the success.

A regular system of exercises of this description is yet a desideratum. But it cannot be difficult for a mother to introduce into the amusements of her children a number of these exercises, calculated to develop and perfect the eye and the ear. For it is desirable that everything of that kind should be treated as an amusement, rather than as anything else. The greatest liberty must prevail, and the whole must be done with a certain cheerfulness, without which all these exercises, as gymnastics themselves, would become dull, pedantic, and ridiculous.

173

It will be well to connect these exercises very early with others tending to form the taste. It seems not to be sufficiently understood that good taste and good feelings are kindred to each other, and that they reciprocally confirm each other. Though the ancients have said that "to study those arts which are suited to a free-born mind soothes the character and takes away the roughness of exterior manners," yet little has been done to open a free access to those enjoyments or accomplishments to all, and especially to the majority of the people. If they must not be expected to be able to give much of their attention to subordinate or ornamental pursuits, while so much of it is engrossed in providing for their first and necessary wants, still this does not furnish a conclusive reason why they should be shut out altogether from every pursuit above the toil of their ordinary vocations.

Yet I know not a more gratifying scene than to see, as I have seen among the poor, a mother spreading around her a spirit of silent but serene enjoyment, diffusing among her children a spring of better feelings, and setting the example of removing everything that might offend the taste, not indeed of a fastidious observer but yet of one used to move in another sphere. It is difficult to describe by what means this can be effected. But I have seen it under circumstances which did not promise to render it even possible.

Of one thing I am certain, that it is only through the true spirit of maternal love that it can be obtained. That feeling, of which I cannot too frequently repeat that it is capable of an elevation to the standard of the very best feelings of human nature, is intimately connected with a happy instinct that will lead to a path equally as remote from listlessness and indolence as it is from artificial refinement. Refinement and fastidiousness may do much, if upheld by constant watchfulness; a nature, however, a truth will be wanting; and even the casual observer will be struck with a restraint incompatible with an atmosphere of sympathy.

Now that I am on the topic, I will not let the opportunity pass by without speaking of one of the most effective aids of moral education. You are aware that I mean *music,* and not only are you acquainted with my sentiments on that subject, but you have also observed the very satisfactory results which we have obtained in our schools. The exertions of my excellent friend Nageli, who has with equal taste and judgment reduced the highest principles of his art to the simplest elements, have enabled us to bring our children to a proficiency which on any other plan must be the work of much time and labor.

But it is not this proficiency which I would describe as a desirable accomplishment of education. It is the marked and most beneficial influence of music on the feelings, which I have always observed to be the most efficient in preparing, or as it were attuning, the mind for the best impressions. The exquisite harmony of a superior performance, the studied elegance of the execution, may indeed give satisfaction to a connoisseur; but it is the simple and untaught grace of melody which speaks to the heart of every human being. Our own national melodies, which have since time immemorial been resounding in our native valleys, are fraught with reminiscences of the brightest page of our history and of the most endearing scenes of domestic life.

But the effect of music in education is not only to keep alive a national feeling: it goes much deeper; if cultivated in the right spirit it strikes at the root of every bad or narrow feeling, of every ungenerous or mean propensity, of every emotion unworthy of humanity.

In saying so I might quote an authority which commands our attention on account of the elevated character and genius of the man from whom it proceeds. It is well-known, that there was not a more eloquent and warm advocate of the moral virtues of music than the venerable Luther. But though his voice has made itself heard and is still held in the highest esteem among us, yet experience has spoken still louder and more unquestionably to the truth of the proposition which he was among the first to vindicate. Experience has long since proved that a system proceeding upon the principle of sympathy would be imperfect if it were to deny itself the assistance of that powerful means of the culture of the heart. Those schools or those families in which music has retained the cheerful and chaste character which it is so important that it should preserve have invariably displayed scenes of moral feeling and consequently of happiness which leave no doubt as to the intrinsic value of that art, which has sunk into neglect or degenerated into abuse only in the ages of barbarism or depravity.

I need not remind you of the importance of music in engendering and assisting the highest feelings of which man is capable. It is almost universally acknowledged that Luther saw the truth when he pointed to music, devoid of studied pomp and vain ornament, in its solemn and impressive simplicity, as one of the most efficient means of elevating and purifying genuine feelings of devotion.

We have frequently in our conversations on this subject been at a loss how to account for the circumstance that in

your own country, though that fact is as generally acknowledged, yet music does not form a more prominent feature
in general education. It would seem that the notion prevails
that it would require more time and application than can
conveniently be bestowed upon it, to make its influence extend also on the education of the people.

Now I would appeal with the same confidence as I would
to yourself to any traveller, whether he has not been struck
with the facility as well as the success with which it is
cultivated among us. Indeed there is scarcely a village
school throughout Switzerland, and perhaps there is none
throughout Germany or Prussia, in which something is not
done for an acquirement of at least the elements of music
on the new and more appropriate plan.

This is a fact which it cannot be difficult to examine, and
which it will be impossible to dispute; and I will conclude
this letter by expressing the hope which we have been
entertaining together, that *this fact will not be overlooked
in a country which has never been backward in suggesting
or adopting improvement when founded on facts, and confirmed by experience.*

LETTER XXIV

February 27, 1819.

MY DEAR GREAVES,

In the branch of education of which I have been treating
in the two last letters, I conceive that to the elements of
music should be subjoined the elements of drawing.

We all know from experience that among the first manifestations of the faculties of a child are a desire and an attempt of imitation. This accounts for the acquirement of

language, and for the first imperfect utterance of sounds imitative of music which is common to most children when they have heard a tune with which they were pleased. The progress in both depends on the greater or smaller portion of attention which children give to the things that surround them, and on their quickness of perception. In the very same way as this applies to the ear and the organs of speech, it applies also to the eye and the employment of the hand. Children who evince some curiosity in the objects brought before their eyes very soon begin to employ their ingenuity and skill in copying what they have seen. Most children will manage to construct something in imitation of a building, of any materials they can lay hold of.

This desire, which is natural to them, should not be neglected. It is like all the faculties capable of regular development. It is therefore well done to furnish children with playthings which will facilitate these their first essays, and occasionally to assist them. No encouragement of that sort is lost upon them; and encouragement should never be withheld when it promotes innocent pleasure and when it may lead to useful occupation. To relieve them from the monotonousness of their daily and hourly repeated trifles, and to introduce variety into their little amusements, acts as a stimulus to their ingenuity and sharpens their observation while it gains their interest.

As soon as they are able to make the attempt there is nothing so well calculated for this object as some elementary practice of drawing.

You have seen the course of preparatory exercises by which some of my friends have so well succeeded in facilitating these pursuits for quite young children. It would be unreasonable to expect that they should begin by drawing any object before them as a whole. It is necessary to analyze for them the parts and elements of which it consists. Whenever this has been attempted the progress has been astonishing, and equalled only by the delight with which the children followed this their favorite pursuit. My friends Ramsauer and Boniface[1] have undertaken the very useful work of arranging such a course in its natural progress from the easiest to the most complicated exercises; and the number of schools in which their method has been successfully practised confirms the experience which we have made at Yverdon of its merits.

The general advantages resulting from an early practice of drawing are evident to every one. Those who are familiar with the art are known to look upon almost every object with eyes different as it were from a common observer. One who is in the habit of examining the structure of plants and conversant with a system of botany will discover a number of distinguishing characteristics of a flower, for instance, which remain wholly unnoticed by one unacquainted with that science. It is from the same reason that even in common life a person who is in the habit of drawing, especially from Nature, will easily perceive many

[1] Both these gentlemen have since published several works, the first in German, and the second in French, with illustrations. Their principles, which were first applied in the Pestalozzian schools, are now very generally adopted in the best schools of Germany and France; and their works, especially that of Ramsauer, would well deserve a translation into English. The superiority of their method has been generally acknowledged by the Englishmen who have seen it practised in the Pestalozzian institutions.

circumstances which are commonly overlooked, and form a much more correct impression even of such objects as he does not stop to examine minutely, than one who has never been taught to look upon what he sees with an intention to reproduce a likeness of it. The attention to the exact shape of the whole and the proportion of the parts which is requisite for the taking of an adequate sketch is converted into a habit, and becomes in many cases productive of much instruction and amusement.

In order to attain this habit, it is material and almost indispensable that children should not be confined to copying from another drawing, but permitted to sketch from Nature. The impression which the object itself gives is so much more striking than its appearance in an imitation that it gives a child much more pleasure to exercise his skill in attempting a likeness of what surrounds him and of what he is interested in, than to labor at a copy of what is but a copy itself, and has less of life or interest in its appearance.

It is likewise much easier to give an idea of the important subject of light and shade and of the first principles of perspective, as far as they influence the representation of every object, by placing it immediately before the eye. The assistance which is given should by no means extend to a direction in the execution of every detail; but something should be left to the ingenuity, something also to patience and perseverance: an advantage that has been found out after some fruitless attempts is not easily forgotten; it gives much satisfaction and encouragement to new efforts; and the joy at the ultimate success derives a zest from previous disappointment.

Next to the exercises of drawing come those of modelling,

in whatever materials may be most conveniently employed. This is frequently productive of even more amusement. Even where there is no distinguished mechanical talent, the pleasure of being able to do something at least is with many a sufficient excitement: and both drawing and modelling, if taught on principles which are founded in nature, will be of the greatest use when the pupils are to enter upon other branches of instruction.

Of these I shall here only mention two—geometry and geography. The preparatory exercises by which we have introduced a course of geometry present an analysis of the various combinations under which the elements of form are brought together, and of which every figure or diagram consists. These elements are already familiar to the pupil who has been taught to consider an object with a view to decompose it into its original parts and to draw them separately. The pupil of course will not be a stranger to the materials of which he is now to be taught the combinations and proportions. It must be easier to understand the properties of a circle, for instance, or of a square, for one who not only has met with these figures occasionally, but is already acquainted with the manner in which they are formed. Besides, the doctrine of geometrical solids, which cannot in any degree be satisfactorily taught without illustrative models, is much better understood and much deeper impressed on the mind when the pupils have some idea of the construction of the models, and when they are able to work out at least those which are less complicated.

In geography, the drawing of outline maps is an exercise which ought not to be neglected in any school. It gives the most accurate idea of the proportional extent and the general position of the different countries; it conveys a more distinct notion than any description, and it leaves the most permanent impression on the memory.

March 5, 1819.

MY DEAR GREAVES,

To the courses of exercises which I have recommended, I anticipate that an objection will be raised which it is necessary for me to meet before I proceed to speak of intellectual education.

Granting that these exercises may be as the phrase is useful in their way; granting even that it might be desirable to see some of the knowledge they are intended to convey diffused among all classes of society; yet where, it will be asked, and by what means can they be expected to become general among any other than the higher classes? There you may expect to find mothers competent, if at all inclined, to undertake the superintendence of such exercises with their children. But considering the present state of things is it not absolutely chimerical to imagine that among the people mothers should be found who are qualified to do anything for their children in that direction?

To this objection I would answer in the first place that it is not always legitimate to conclude from the present state of things to the future; and whenever as in the case before us the present state of things can be proved to be faulty and at the same time capable of improvement, every friend of humanity will concur with me in saying that such a conclusion is inadmissible.

It is inadmissible; for experience speaks against it. The

page of history to a thinking observer presents mankind laboring under the influence of a chain of prejudice of which the links are successively broken.

The most interesting events in history are but the consummation of things which had been deemed impossible. It is in vain to assign limits to the improvements of ingenuity; *but it is still more so to circumscribe the exertions of benevolence.*

Such a conclusion then is inadmissible. And history speaks more directly to the point. The most consequential facts plead in favor of our wishes and our hopes. The most enlightened, the most active philanthropists, two thousand years ago, could not have foreseen the change that has taken place in the intellectual world: they could not have anticipated those facilities by which not only is the research of a few encouraged, but the practical results of that research are with wonderful rapidity communicated to thousands in the remotest countries of the globe. They could not have foreseen the glorious invention by which ignorance and superstition have been driven out of their stronghold, and knowledge and truth diffused in the most universal and the most effective channels. They could not have foreseen that a spirit of inquiry would be excited even among those who had formerly been doomed to blind belief and to passive obedience.

Indeed, if there is one feature by which this present age bids fair to redeem its character and to heal the wounds which it has inflicted on the suffering nations it is this— that we see efforts making in every direction with a zeal and to an extent hitherto unparallelled to assist the people in acquiring that portion of intellectual independence without which the true dignity of the human character cannot be maintained nor its duties adequately fulfilled. There is something so cheering in the prospect of seeing the number of those for whom it is destined extending with the range of knowledge itself, that there is scarcely a field left of which men of superior talent have not undertaken to cull the flowers and to store the fruits for those who have not time or faculty to toil at the elements or follow up the refinements of science; and the still more material object, to facilitate the first steps, to lay the foundation, to ensure the slow but solid progress, and to do this in the manner best adapted to the nature of the human mind, and to the development of its faculties: this object has been pursued with an interest and an ardor that even the results which I have seen in my own immediate neighborhood are a sufficient pledge that the pursuit will not be abandoned, and that it is now not far from its ultimate success.

This prospect is cheering: but, my dear friend, it is not upon this prospect that I have built the hopes of my life. It is not the diffusion of knowledge, whether it be grudgingly doled out in schools on the old plan, or more liberally supplied in establishments on a new principle, or submitted to the examination, and laid open for the improvement of the adults; it is not the diffusion of knowledge alone to which I look up for the welfare of this or any generation. No: unless we succeed in giving a new impulse, and raising the tone of *Domestic Education;* unless an atmosphere of sympathy, elevated by moral and religious feeling, be diffused there; unless material love be rendered more instrumental in early education than any other agent; unless mothers will consent to follow the call of their own better feelings more readily than those of pleasure or of thought-less habit; unless they will consent to be mothers, and to act as mothers—unless such· be the character of education, all our hopes and exertions can end only in disappointment.

Those have indeed widely mistaken the meaning of all my plans and of those of my friends who suppose that in our labors for popular education we have not a higher end in view than the improvement of a system of instruction, or the perfection as it were of the gymnastics of the intel-lect. We have been busily engaged in reforming the schools, for we consider them as essential in the progress of edu-cation: but we consider the fireside circle as far more es-sential. We have done all in our power to bring up chil-dren with a view to become teachers, and we have every reason to congratulate the schools that were benefited by this plan: but we have thought it the most important fea-ture and the first duty of our own schools and of every school, to develop in the pupils confided to our care those feelings and to store their minds with that knowledge which, at a more advanced period of life, may enable them to give all their heart and the unwearied use of their powers to the diffusion of the true spirit which should prevail in a domestic circle. In short, whoever has the welfare of the rising generation at heart cannot do better than consider as his highest object the *Education of Mothers.*

LETTER XXVI

March 15, 1819.

MY DEAR GREAVES,

Let me repeat that we cannot expect any real improve-ment in education that shall be felt throughout an extensive sphere and that shall continue to spread in the progress of time, increasing in vigor as it proceeds, unless we begin by *educating mothers*.

It is their duty in the domestic circle to do what school instruction has not the means of accomplishing; to give to every individual child that degree of attention which in a school is absorbed in the management of the whole; to let their heart speak in cases where the heart is the best judge; to gain by affection what authority could never have commanded.

But it is their duty also to turn all the stock of their knowledge to account, and to let their children have the benefit of it.

I am aware that under the present circumstances many mothers would either declare themselves or would be looked upon by others as incompetent to attempt any such thing; as so poor in knowledge and so unpractised in communicating knowledge that such an undertaking on their part would appear as vain and presumptuous.

Now this is a fact, which, as far as experience goes, I am bound to deny. I am not now speaking of those classes or individuals whose education has been if not very diligently at least in some measure attended to. I have now in view a mother whose education has from some circumstances or other been totally neglected. I will suppose one who is even ignorant of reading and writing, though in no country in which the schools are in a proper state would you meet with an individual deficient in this respect. I will add, a young and inexperienced mother.

Now I will venture to say that this poor and wholly ignorant, this young and inexperienced mother, is *not quite destitute* of the means of assisting even in the intellectual development of her child.

However small may be the stock of her experience, however moderate her own faculties, she must be aware that she is acquainted with an infinite number of facts, such we will say as they occur in common life, to which her infant is yet a stranger. She must be aware that it will be useful to the infant to become soon acquainted with some of them, such for instance as refer to things with which it is likely to come into contact. She must feel herself able to give her child the possession of a variety of names, simply by bringing the objects themselves before the child, pronouncing the names, and making the child repeat them. She must feel herself able to bring such objects before the child in a sort of natural order—the different parts for instance of a fruit. Let no one despise these things because they are little. There was a time when we were ignorant even of the least of them; and there are those to whom we have reason to be thankful for teaching us these little things.

But I do not mean to say that a mother should stop there. Even the mother of whom we are speaking, that wholly ignorant and inexperienced mother, is capable of going much farther, and of adding a variety of knowledge which is really useful. After she has exhausted the stock of objects which presented themselves first, after the child has acquired the names of them, and is able to distinguish their parts, it may probably occur to her that something more might still be said on every one of these objects. She will find herself able to describe them to the child with regard to form, size, color, softness or hardness of the outside, sound when touched, and so on.

She has now gained a material point; from the mere knowledge of the names of objects, she has led the infant to a knowledge of their qualities and properties. Nothing can be more natural for her than to go on and compare different objects with regard to these qualities, and the greater or smaller degree in which they belong to the objects. If the former exercises were adapted to cultivate the memory, these are calculated to form the observation and judgment.

She may still go much farther: she is able to tell her child the reasons of things, and the causes of facts. She is able to inform it of the origin and the duration and the consequences of a variety of objects. The occurrences of every day and of every hour will furnish her with materials for this sort of instruction. Its use is evident; it teaches the child to inquire after the causes, and accustoms it to think of the consequences of things.

I shall have an opportunity in another place to speak of moral and religious instruction; I will therefore only remark in a few words that this last-mentioned class of exercises, which may be varied and extended in an almost endless series, will give frequent occasion for the simplest illustration of truths belonging to that branch. It will make the child reflect on the consequences of actions; it will render the mind familiar with thought; and it will frequently lead to recognize in the objects before the child the effects of the infinite wisdom of that Being whom long before the piety of the mother if genuine must have led him to revere and to love "with all his heart, and with all his soul, and with all his strength, and with all his mind."

I am afraid that the enumeration of these first essays of a mother will be found tedious by other readers than yourself, whom I have never seen weary of watching nature and drawing instruction from the inexhaustible spring of experience. I think that we sympathize on this subject; that we feel greater interest in the unsophisticated consciousness of a pure intention than in the most splendid exhibition of refinement of knowledge.

And I know not a motive which might render those efforts more interesting than the desire of a mother to do all in her power for the mental as well as the physical and moral development of her children. However circumscribed her means, and however limited at first may be her success, still there is something that will and must prompt her not to rest, that will stimulate her to new efforts, and that will at last crown them with fruits which are the more gratifying, the more they were difficult to obtain.

Experience has shown that mothers in that seemingly forlorn situation which I have described have succeeded beyond their own expectation. I look upon this as a new proof of the fact that nothing is too difficult for maternal love, animated by a consciousness of its purity, and elevated by a confidence in the power of Him who has inspired the mother's heart with that feeling. I do indeed consider it as a free gift of the Creator, and I firmly believe that in the same measure as maternal love is ardent and indefatigable, in the same measure as it is inspired with energy and enhanced by faith—I firmly believe that in the same measure maternal love will be strengthened in its exertions, and supplied with means, even where it appears most destitute.

Though, as I have shown above, it is by no means so difficult to direct the attention of children to useful objects, yet nothing is more common than the complaint, "I can do nothing with children." If this comes from an individual who is not called upon by his peculiar situation to occupy himself with education, it is but fair to suppose that he will be able to make himself more useful in another direction than he could have done by a laborious and persevering application to a task for which he is neither predisposed by inclination nor fitted by eminent talent. But those words should never come from a mother. A mother *is* called upon to give her attention to that subject. It is her duty to do so; the voice of conscience in her own breast will tell her that it is. The consciousness of a duty never exists without the qualification to fulfil it; nor has a duty ever been undertaken with the spirit of courage, of confidence, of love, that has not been ultimately crowned with success.

LETTER XXVII

March 20, 1819.

My dear Greaves,

If even an uneducated and totally unassisted mother has it in her power to do so much for her child, how much better qualified must she be, and how much more confidently may she look forward to the results of her maternal exertions, if her faculties have been properly developed, and her steps guided by the experience of those who had engaged in that work before her.

The fact therefore which I stated in my last letter, far from rendering my proposition questionable, goes directly to confirm its validity and to illustrate its expediency. I therefore repeat it, and I would address it in the strongest language to all those who like myself are desirous of bringing about a change in our present insufficient system of education. If you really wish to embark with your facilities, your time, your talents, your influence, in a cause likely to benefit a large portion of your species—if you wish not to be busy in suggesting palliatives but in effecting a permanent cure of the evils under which thousands have sunk and hundreds of thousands are still suffering; if you wish not merely to erect an edifice that may attract by its splendor and commemorate your name for a while, but which shall pass away like "the baseless fabric of vision"; but if on the contrary you prefer solid improvement to momentary effect, and the lasting benefit of many to the solitary gratification of striking results; let not your attention be diverted by the apparent wants—let it not be totally engrossed by the subordinate ones—but let it at once be directed to the great and general though little known source from which good or evil flows in quantity incalculable and rapidity unparallelled—to the manner in which the earliest years of childhood are passed, and to the education of those to whose care they are or ought to be consigned.

Of all institutions, the most useful is one in which the great business of education is not merely made a means subservient to the various purposes of ordinary life, but in which it is viewed as an object in itself deserving of the most serious attention and to be brought to the highest perfection; a school in which the pupils are taught to act as teachers and educated to act as educators; a school, above all, in which the *female character* is at an early period developed in that direction which enables it to take so prominent a part in early education.

To effect this it is necessary that the female character should be thoroughly understood and adequately appreciated. And on this subject nothing can give a more satisfactory illustration than the observation of a mother who is conscious of her duties and qualified to fulfil them. In such a mother the moral dignity of her character, the suavity of her manners, and the firmness of her principles will not more command our admiration, than the happy mixture of judgment and feeling which constitutes the simple but unerring standard of her actions.

It is the great problem in female education to effect this happy union in the mind, which is equally as far from imposing any restraint on the feelings as it is from warping or biasing the judgment. The marked preponderance of feeling which is manifested in the female character requires not only the most clearsighted but also the kindest attention from those who wish to bring it into harmony with the development of the faculties of the intellect and the will.

It is a mere prejudice to suppose that the acquirement of knowledge and the cultivation of the intellect, must either not be solid and comprehensive, or must take away from the female character its simplicity and all that renders it truly amiable. Every thing depends on the motive from which and the spirit in which knowledge is acquired. Let that motive be one that does honor to human nature, and let that spirit be the same which is concomitant to all the graces of the female character,

Not obvious, not obtrusive,—but retired,

and there will be modesty to ensure solidity of knowledge, and delicacy to guard against the misdirection of sentiment.

For an example, I might refer to one of the numerous instances which are not the less striking because they are not extensively known, in which a mother has devoted much of her time and best abilities to the acquirement of some branches of knowledge in which her own education had been defective, but which she conceived to be valuable enough to be brought forward in the education of her own children. This has been the case with individuals highly accomplished in many respects, but still alive to every defect and desirous of supplying it, if not for their own at least for the benefit of their children.

And no mother has ever been known to have repented of any pains that she took to qualify herself for the most perfect education of those nearest and dearest to her heart. Even without anticipating the future accomplishment of her wishes by their progress in which she has undertaken to guide them she is amply repaid by the delight immediately arising from the task,

to rear the tender thought,
And teach the young idea how to shoot.

I have here supposed the most powerful motive, that of maternal love; but it will be the task of early education to supply motives which even at a tender age may excite an interest in mental exertion, and yet be allied to the best feelings of human nature.

PESTALOZZI

March 27, 1819.

MY DEAR GREAVES,

If a mother is desirous of taking an active part in the intellectual education of her children, I would first direct her attention to the necessity of considering, not only what sort of knowledge, but in what manner that knowledge should be communicated to the infant mind. For her purpose the latter consideration is even more essential than the former; for however excellent the information may be which she wishes to impart, it will depend on the mode of her doing it whether it will at all gain access to the mind, or whether it will remain unprofitable, neither suiting the faculties nor being apt to excite the interest of the child.

In this respect a mother should be able perfectly to distinguish between the mere action of the memory and that of the other faculties of the mind.

To the want of this distinction I think we may safely ascribe much of the waste of time and the deceptive exhibition of apparent knowledge which is so frequent in schools, both of a higher and a lower character. It is a mere fallacy to conclude or to pretend that knowledge has been acquired, from the circumstance that terms have been committed to the memory which, if rightly understood, convey the expression of knowledge. This condition, *if rightly understood,* which is the most material is the most generally overlooked. No doubt a proceeding of this sort, when words are committed to the memory without an adequate explanation being either given or required is the most commodious evidence for the indolence or ignorance of those who practise upon it as a system of instruction. Add to which the powerful stimulus of vanity in the pupils, the hope of distinction and reward in some, the fear of exposure or punishment in others, and we shall have the principal motives before us owing to which this system in spite of its wretchedness has so long been patronized by those who do not think at all, and tolerated by those who do not sufficiently think for themselves.

What I have said just now of the exercise of the memory exclusive of a well-regulated exercise of the understanding, applies more especially to the manner in which the dead languages have long been and in some places still are taught; a system of which, taking it all in all, with its abstruse and unintelligible rules and its compulsive discipline, it is difficult to say whether it is more absurd in an intellectual, or more detestable in a moral point of view.

If such a system, enforcing the partial exercise of the memory, is so absurd in its application and so detrimental in its consequences, at a period when the intellect may be supposed to be able to make some progress at least without being so constantly and anxiously attended to, an exclusive cultivation of the memory must be still more misapplied at the tender age when the intellect is only just dawning, when the faculty of discerning is yet unformed and unable to consign to the memory the notions of separate objects in their distinction from each other. For a mother to guard against an error of this kind the first rule is to teach always by *things* rather than by *words*. Let there be as few objects as possible named to the infant unless you are prepared to show the objects themselves. When you can show the object the name will be committed to the memory, together with the recollection of the impression which the object produced on the senses. It is an old saying, and a very true one, that our attention is much more forcibly attracted and more permanently fixed by objects which have been brought before our eyes than by others of which we have merely gathered some notion from hearsay and description or from the mention of a name.

But if a mother is to teach by *things,* she must recollect also that to the formation of an idea more is requisite than the bringing of the object before the senses. Its qualities must be explained; its origin must be accounted for; its parts must be described, and their relation to the whole ascertained; its use, its effects or consequences, must be stated. All this must be done in a manner at least sufficiently clear and comprehensive to enable the child to distinguish the object from other objects and to account for the distinction which is made.

It is natural that the degree of perfection with which the formation of ideas on this plan can be facilitated depends upon circumstances which are not always under the control of a mother; but something of the kind should be attempted and must be, wherever education is intended to take a higher character than mere mechanical training of the memory.

Of objects which cannot be brought before the child in reality, pictures should be introduced. Instruction founded on pictures will always be found a favorite branch with children, and if this curiosity is well directed and judiciously satisfied it will prove one of the most useful and instructive.

Whenever the knowledge of an abstract idea, which will

not of course admit of any representation of that kind, is to be communicated to the child, on the same principle an equivalent of that representation should be given by an exemplification through the medium of a fact laid before the child. This is the original intention and the use of moral tales; and, this, too, agrees with the excellent old adage, "The way by precept is long and laborious, that by example short and easy."

LETTER XXIX

April 4, 1819.

My dear Greaves,

The second rule that I would give to a mother, respecting the early development of the infant mind is this: Let the child not only be *acted upon* but let him be an *agent* in intellectual education.

I shall explain my meaning. Let the mother bear in mind that her child has not only the faculties of attention to and retention of certain ideas or facts, but also a faculty of reflection, independent of the thoughts of others. It is well done to make a child read, and write, and learn, and repeat, —but it is still better to make a child *think*. We may be able to turn to account the opinions of others, and we may find it valuable or advantageous to be acquainted with them; we may profit by their light; but we can render ourselves most useful to others and we shall be most entitled to the character of valuable members of society by the efforts of our own minds; by the result of our own investigations; by those views and their application which we may call our own intellectual property.

I am not now speaking of those leading ideas which are

from time to time thrown out, and by which science is advanced or society benefited at large. I am speaking of that stock of intellectual property which every one may acquire, even the most unpretending individual and in the humblest walks of life. I am speaking of that habit of reflection which guards against unthinking conduct under any circumstances, and which is always active to examine that which is brought before the mind; that habit of reflection which excludes the self-sufficiency of ignorance or the levity of "a little learning"; which may lead an individual to the modest acknowledgement that he knows but little, and to the honest consciousness that he knows that little well. To engender this habit, nothing is so effective as an early development in the infant mind of thought—regular self-active thought.

Let not the mother suffer herself to be detained from this task by the objections of those who deem the infant mind altogether incapable of any exertion of that kind. I will venture to say that those who propose that objection, though they may be the profoundest thinkers or the greatest theorists, will be found to have no *practical* knowledge whatsoever of the subject nor any moral interest in the investigation of it. And I, for one, would trust more in the experimental knowledge of a mother, proceeding from exertions to which she was prompted by maternal feeling— in that experimental knowledge, even of an illiterate mother, I would trust more than in the theoretical speculations of the most ingenious philosophers. There are cases in which sound sense and a warm heart see farther than a highly refined, cold, and calculating head.

I would therefore call upon the mother to begin her task,

in spite of any objections that may be raised. It will be enough if she is persuaded to *begin;* she will then continue of herself; she will derive such gratification from her task that she will never think of relaxing.

While she unfolds the treasures of the infant mind and uncloses the world of hitherto slumbering thought, she will not envy the assurance of philosophers who would have the human mind to be a "universal blank." Engaged in a task which calls into activity all the energies of her mind and all the affections of her heart, she will smile at their dictatorial speculations and their supercilious theories. Without troubling herself about the knotty question whether there are any *innate ideas,* she will be content if she succeeds in developing the *innate faculties of the mind.*

If a mother asks for the designation of the subjects which might be profitably used as vehicles for the development of thought, I would answer her that any subject will do if it be treated in a manner suitable to the faculties of the child. It is the great art in teaching, never to be at a loss for the choice of an object for the illustration of a truth. There is not an object so trivial that in the hands of a skilful teacher it might not become interesting, if not from its own nature, at least from the mode of treating it. To a child everything is new. The charm of novelty, it is true, soon wears off; and if there is not the fastidiousness of matured years there is at least the impatience of infancy to contend with. But then there is for the teacher the great advantage of a combination of simple elements, which may diversify the subject without dividing the attention.

If I say that any subject will do for the purpose, I mean this to be understood literally. Not only there is not one of

the little incidents in the life of a child, in his amusements
and recreations, in his relations to his parents and friends
and playfellows, but there is not actually anything within
the reach of the child's attention, whether it belong to nature or to the employments and arts of life, that might not
be made the object of a lesson by which some useful knowledge might be imparted, and, which is still more important,
by which the child might not be familiarized with the
habit of thinking on what he sees and speaking after he
has thought.

The mode of doing this is not by any means to talk
much *to* a child, but to enter into conversation *with* a child;
not to address to him many words, however familiar or
well chosen, but to bring him to express himself on the
subject; not to exhaust the subject, but to question the child
about it, and to let him find out and correct the answers.
It would be ridiculous to expect that the volatile spirits of
an infant could be brought to follow any lengthy explanations. The attention of a child is deadened by long expositions but roused by animated questions.

Let these questions be short, clear, and intelligible. Let
them not merely lead the child to repeat in the same or in
varied terms what he has heard just before. Let them excite
him to observe what is before him, to recollect what he has
learned, and to muster his little stock of knowledge for
materials for an answer. Show him a certain quality in one
thing, and let him find out the same in others. Tell him
that the shape of a ball is called round; and if, accordingly,
you bring him to point out other objects to which the same
character belongs you have employed him more usefully
than by the most perfect discourse on rotundity. In the one

instance he would have had to listen and to recollect; in the other he has to observe and to think.

April 10, 1819.

MY DEAR GREAVES,

When I recommend to a mother to avoid *wearying* a child by her instructions, I do not wish to encourage the notion that instruction should always take the character of an amusement or even of play. I am convinced that such a notion where it is entertained and acted upon by a teacher will forever preclude solidity of knowledge, and from a want of sufficient exertion on the part of the pupils will lead to that very result which I wish to avoid by my principle of a constant employment of the thinking powers.

A child must very early in life be taught a lesson which frequently comes too late and is then a most painful one— that exertion is indispensable for the attainment of knowledge. But a child should not be taught to look upon exertion as an unavoidable *evil*. The motive of *fear* should not be made a stimulus to exertion. It will destroy the interest and will speedily create disgust.

This *interest* in study is the first thing which a teacher, and in the instances before us, which a mother should endeavor to excite and keep alive. There are scarcely any circumstances in which a want of application in children does not proceed from a want of interest; and there are perhaps none under which a want of interest does not originate in the mode of treating adopted by the teacher. I would go so far as to lay it down for a rule that whenever children are inattentive and apparently take no interest in a lesson, the teacher should always first look to himself for the reason. When a quantity of dry matter is before a child, when a child is doomed to listen in silence to lengthy explanations or to go through exercises which have nothing in themselves to relieve or attract the mind, this is a tax upon his spirits which a teacher should make it a point to abstain from imposing. In the same manner if the child from the imperfection of his reasoning powers or his unacquaintance with facts is unable to enter into the sense or to follow the chain of ideas in a lesson, when he is made to hear or to repeat what to him is but "sound without sense"—this is perfectly absurd. And when to all this the fear of punishment is added—besides the tedium, which in itself is punishment enough—this becomes absolutely cruel.

Of all tyrants, it is well known that little tyrants are the most cruel; and of all little tyrants the most cruel are *school tyrants*. Now in all civilized countries cruelty of every description is forbidden, and even cruelty to animals is properly punished, in some by the law of the land, and in all stigmatized by public opinion. How then comes *cruelty to children* to be so generally overlooked, or rather thought a matter of course?

Some, forsooth, will tell us that their own measures are wonderfully humane, that their punishments are less severe, or that they have done away with corporal punishments. But it is not to the severity of them that I object—nor would I venture to assert in an unqualified manner that corporal punishments are inadmissible under any circumstances in education. But I do object to their application—I do object to the principle *that the children are punished when the master or the system is to blame.*

THE LETTERS TO GREAVES

As long as this shall continue—as long as teachers will not take the trouble or will not be found qualified to inspire their pupils with a living interest in their studies—they must not complain of the want of attention nor even of the aversion to instruction which some of them may manifest. Could we witness the indescribable tedium which must oppress the juvenile mind while the weary hours are slowly passing away, one by one, in an occupation which they can neither relish nor understand its use; could we remember the same scenes which our own childhood has undergone, we should then no longer be surprised at the remissness of the school-boy, "creeping, like snail, unwillingly to school."

In saying this I do not mean to make myself the advocate of idleness or of those irregularities which will now and then be met with even in the best conducted schools. But I would suggest that the best means to prevent them from becoming general is to adopt a better mode of instruction, by which the children are less left to themselves, less thrown upon the unwelcome employment of passive listening, less harshly treated for little and excusable failings, but more roused by questions, animated by illustrations, interested and won by kindness.

There is a most remarkable reciprocal action between the interest which the teacher takes and that which he communicates to his pupils. If he is not with his whole mind present at the subject; if he does not care whether it is understood or not, whether his manner is liked or not, he will never fail of alienating the affections of his pupils, and of rendering them indifferent to what he says. But real interest taken in the task of instruction—kind words, and kinder feelings—the very expression of the features, and the glance of the eye, are never lost upon children.

April 17, 1819.

My dear Greaves,

You are aware of the nature of those exercises which were adopted at my suggestion as calculated to employ the mind usefully and to prepare it for further pursuits by eliciting thought and forming the intellect.

I would call them preparatory exercises in more than one respect. They embrace the elements of number, form, and language; and whatever ideas we may have to acquire in the course of our life, they are all introduced through the medium of one of these three departments.

The relations and proportions of number and form constitute the natural measure of all those impressions which the mind receives without. They are the measures of and comprehend the qualities of the material world, form being the measure of space, and number the measure of time. Two or more objects distinguished from each other as existing separately in space, pre-suppose an idea of their forms, or in other words, of the exact space which they occupy; distinguished from each other as existing at different times, they come under the denomination of number.

The reason why I would so early call the attention of children to the elements of number and form is, besides their general usefulness, that they admit of a most perspicuous treatment—a treatment of course far different from that in which they are but too often involved, and rendered utterly unpalatable to those who are by no means deficient in abilities.

The elements of number, or preparatory exercises of Calculation, should always be taught by submitting to the eye of the child certain objects representing the units. A child can conceive the idea of two balls, two roses, two books; but it cannot conceive the idea of "Two" in the abstract. How would you make the child understand that two and two make four, unless you show it to him first in reality? To begin by abstract notions is absurd and detrimental, instead of being educative. The result is at best that the child can do the thing by rote without understanding it; a fact which does not reflect on the child but on the teacher, who knows not a higher character of instruction than mere mechanical training.

If the elements are thus clearly and intelligibly taught, it will always be easy to go on to more difficult parts, remembering always that the whole should be done by *questions*. As soon as you have given to the child a knowledge of the names by which the numbers are distinguished, you may appeal to it to answer any question of simple addition or subtraction or multiplication or division, performing the operation in reality by means of a certain number of objects, balls for instance, which will serve in the place of units.

It has been objected that children who had been used to a constant and palpable exemplification of the units by which they were enabled to execute the solution of arithmetical questions, would never be able afterwards to follow the problems of calculation in the abstract, their balls or other representatives being taken from them.

Now experience has shown that those very children who had acquired the first elements in the palpable and familiar method described had two great advantages over others. First, they were perfectly aware not only of what they were doing but also of the reason why. They were acquainted with the principle on which the solution depended; they were not merely following a formula by rote; the state of the question changed they were not puzzled, as those are who see only as far as their mechanical rule goes and not farther. This, while it produced confidence and a feeling of safety, gave them also much delight—a difficulty overcome with a consciousness of a felicitous effort always prompts to the undertaking of a new one.

The second advantage was that children well versed in those illustrative elementary exercises afterwards displayed great skill in mental arithmetic. Without repairing to their slate or paper, without making any memorandum of figures, they not only performed operations with large numbers, but they arranged and solved questions which at first might have appeared involved, even had the assistance of memoranda or working out on paper been allowed.

Of the numerous travellers of your nation who did me the honor to visit my establishment, there was none, however little he might be disposed or qualified to enter into a consideration of the whole of my plan, who did not express his astonishment at the perfect ease and the quickness with which arithmetical problems, such as the visitors used to propose, were solved. I do not mention this and I did not feel then any peculiar satisfaction on account of the display with which it was connected, though the acknowledgment of strangers can by no means be indifferent to one who wishes to see his plan judged of by its results. But the reason why I felt much interested and gratified by the impression which that department of the school invariably produced was that it singularly confirmed the fitness and utility of our elementary course. It went a great way at least with me to make me hold fast the principle that the infant mind should be acted upon by illustrations taken from reality, not by rules taken from abstraction; that we ought to teach by *things* more than by *words.*

In the exercises concerning the elements of form my friends have most successfully revived and extended what the ancients called the *analytical method*—the mode of eliciting facts by problems, instead of stating them in theories; of elucidating the origin of them, instead of merely commenting on their existence; of leading the mind to invent, instead of resting satisfied with the inventions of others. So truly beneficial, so stimulating is that employment to the mind, that we have learned fully to appreciate the principle of Plato that whoever wished to apply with success to metaphysics ought to prepare himself by the study of geometry. It is not the acquaintance with certain qualities or proportions, of certain forms and figures (though, for many purposes, this is applicable in practical life, and conducive to the advancement of science), but it is the precision of reasoning, and the ingenuity of invention, which, springing as it does from a familiarity with those exercises, qualifies the intellect for exertion of every kind.

In exercises of number and form less abstraction is at first required than in similar ones in language. But I would insist on the necessity of a careful instruction in the maternal language. Of foreign tongues or of the dead languages I think that they ought to be studied by all means by those to whom a knowledge of them may become useful, or who are so circumstanced that they may indulge a predilection for them if their taste or habits lead that way. But I know not of one single exception that I would make of the principle that as early as possible a child should be led to contract an intimate acquaintance with and make himself perfectly master of his native tongue.

Charles the Fifth used to say that as many languages as a man possessed, so often was he man. How far this may be true I will not inquire: but this much I know to be a fact, that the mind is deprived of its first instrument or organ, as it were; that its functions are interrupted and its ideas confused, when there is a want of perfect acquaintance and mastery of at least *one language*. The friends of oppression, of darkness, of prejudice, cannot do better, nor have they at any time neglected the point, than to stifle the power and facility of free, manly, and well-practised speaking; nor can the friends of light and liberty do better, and it were desirable that they were more assiduous in the cause, than to procure to everyone, to the poorest as well as to the richest, a facility if not of elegance at least of frankness and energy of speech—a facility which would enable them to collect and clear up their vague ideas, to embody those which are distinct, and which would awaken a thousand new ones.

THE LETTERS TO GREAVES

April 25, 1819.

My dear Greaves,

Need I point out to you the motive from which I have said thus much on the early attention to be paid to physical and intellectual education? Need I remind you, that I consider these branches merely as leading to a higher aim—to qualify the human being for the free and full use of all the faculties implanted by the Creator—and to direct all these faculties towards the perfection of the whole being of man, that he may be enabled to act in his peculiar station as an instrument of that all-wise and almighty Power that has called him into life? This is the view which Education should lead an individual to take of his relation to his Maker—a view which will at once give him humility to acknowledge the imperfection of his attempts and the weakness of his power—and inspire him with the courage of an unshaken confidence in the source of all that is good and true.

In relation to society, man should be qualified by education to be a useful member of it. In order to be truly useful, it is necessary that he should be truly *independent*. Whether that independence may arise from his circumstances, or whether it be acquired by the honorable use of his talents, or whether it be owing to more laborious exertion and frugal habits, it is clear that true independence must rise and fall with the dignity of his moral character, rather than with affluent circumstances or intellectual superiority or indefatigable exertion. A state of bondage or of self-merited poverty is not more degrading than a state of dependence on considerations which betray littleness of mind, or want of moral energy or of honorable feeling. An individual whose actions bear the stamp of independence of mind cannot but be a useful as well as an esteemed member of society. He fills up a certain place in society, belonging to himself and no other, because he has obtained it by merit and secured it by character. His talents, his time, his opportunities, and his influence are all given to a certain end. And even in the humbler walks of life, it has always been acknowledged that there were individuals who by the intelligent, the frank, the honorable character of their demeanor, and by the meritorious tendency of their exertions, deserved to be mentioned together with those whose names were illustrated by the halo of noble birth, and by the still brighter glory of genius or merit. That such instances are but exceptions, and that these exceptions are so few, is owing to the system of education which generally prevails, and which is little calculated to promote independence of character.

Considering man as an individual, education should contribute toward giving him *happiness*. The feeling of happiness does not arise from exterior circumstances; it is a state of the mind, a consciousness of harmony both with the inward and the outward world: it assigns their due limits to the desires, and it proposes the highest aim to the faculties of man. For happy is he who can bring his desires within the measure of his means, and who can resign every individual and selfish wish without giving up his content and repose—whose feeling of general satisfaction is not dependent on individual gratification. And happy again is he who, whenever self is out of the question and the higher perfection of his better nature or the best interests of his race are at stake—happy is he who then knows of no limits to his efforts, and who can bring them to keep pace with his most sanguine hopes! The sphere of happiness is unbounded; it is extending as the views are enlarged; it is elevated as the feelings of the heart are raised; it "grows with their growth, and strengthens with their strength."

In order to give the character described here to the actions and to the life of an individual, I consider it as necessary that all the faculties implanted in human nature should be properly developed. It is not that *virtuosity* ought to be attained in any direction, or that a degree of excellence ought to be anxiously aspired to which is the exclusive privilege of pre-eminent talent. But there is a degree of development of all the faculties which is far from the refinement of any; and of such a course the great advantage will be to prepare the mind for a more especial application to any line of studies congenial to its inclination, or connected with certain pursuits.[1]

With regard to the claim which every human being has to a judicious development of his faculties by those to whom the care of his infancy is confided, a claim of which the universality does not seem to be sufficiently acknowledged, allow me to make use of an illustration which was on one occasion proposed by one of my friends. Whenever we find

[1] What Locke has said more generally of education is strictly applicable to a course of exercises such as have been alluded to in the foregoing pages: "The business of education, in respect of knowledge, is not to perfect the learner in all or any one of the sciences; but to give his mind that disposition, and those habits, that may enable him to attain any part of knowledge he shall stand in need of in the future course of his life."

a human being in a state of suffering, and near to the awful moment which is for ever to close the scene of his pains and his enjoyments in this world, we feel ourselves moved by a sympathy which reminds us that however low his earthly condition, here too there is one of our race, subject to the same sensations of alternate joy and grief, born with the same faculties, with the same destination, with the same hopes for a life of immortality. And as we give ourselves up to that idea, we would fain if we could alleviate his sufferings and shed a ray of light on the darkness of his parting moments. This is a feeling which will come home to the heart of every one, even to the young and the thoughtless, and to those little used to the sight of woe. Why then, we would ask, do we look with a careless indifference on those who enter life? Why do we feel so little interest in the feelings and in the condition of those who enter upon that varied scene, of which, if we would but stop to reflect, we might contribute to enhance the enjoyments, and to diminish the sum of suffering, of discontent and wretchedness? And that education might do that, is the conviction of all those who are competent to speak from experience. That it *ought* to do as much is the persuasion, and that it *may some time* accomplish it is the constant endeavor of all those who are truly interested in the welfare of mankind.

LETTER XXXIII

May 1, 1819.

MY DEAR GREAVES,

In my last letter I described the end of education to be to render man conscientiously active in the service of his Maker; to render him useful by rendering him independent with relation to society; and, as an individual, to render him happy within himself.

To this end I conceive that the formation of the intellect, the attainment of useful knowledge, and the development of all the faculties may be made instrumental. But though they will be found highly serviceable as furnishing the means, they will not supply the spring of action. It would be preposterous, no doubt, to provide for the facilities of execution, without exciting the motives of a certain plan or line of conduct.

Of this fault, the process which frequently goes by the name of education and which might more appropriately be denominated a mechanical training, is often guilty. The common motive by which such a system acts on those whose indolence it has conquered is *Fear;* the very highest to which it can aspire in those whose sensibility is excited is *Ambition.*

It is obvious that such a system can calculate only on the lower selfishness of man. To that least amiable or estimable part of the human character it is, and always has been, indebted for its best success. Upon the better feelings of man it turns a deaf ear.

How is it then that motives leading to a course of action which is looked upon as mean and despicable or at best as doubtful, when it occurs in life, are thought honorable in education? Why should that bias be given to the mind in a school which to gain the respect or the affection of others an individual must first of all strive to unlearn; a bias to which every candid mind is a stranger?

I do not wish to speak harshly of ambition or to reject it altogether as a motive. There is, to be sure, a noble ambition—dignified by its object, and distinguished by a deep and transcendent interest in that object. But if we consider the sort of ambition commonly proposed to the school-boy —if we analyze "what stuff 'tis made of, whereof it is born," we shall find that it has nothing to do with the interest taken in the object of study; that such an interest frequently does not exist; and that, owing to its being blended with that vilest and meanest of motives, with *fear,* it is by no means raised by the wish to give pleasure to those who propose it; for a teacher who proceeds on a system in which fear and ambition are the principal agents must give up his claim to the esteem or the affection of his pupils.

Motives like fear or inordinate ambition may stimulate to exertion, intellectual or physical, but they cannot warm the heart. There is not in them that life which makes the heart of youth to heave with the delight of knowledge, with the honest consciousness of talent, with the honorable wish for distinction, with the kindly glow of genuine feeling. Such motives are inadequate in their source and inefficient in their application; for they are nothing to the heart, and "out of the heart are the issues of life."

On these grounds it is that in moral as well as intellectual education I have urged the supreme character of the motive of sympathy as the one that should early and indeed principally be employed in the management of children. On these grounds I have repeatedly urged the propriety of attending to that feeling which I have no hesitation in declaring to be the first feeling of an higher nature that is alive in the child—the feeling in the infant of love and confidence in the mother. Upon this feeling I wish to ground the first foundation—and on a feeling analogous to it and springing from it I wish to guide the future steps of education.

That in the infant that feeling exists there can be no doubt. We have for it the testimony of those who are most competent to judge, because best enabled to sympathize with it—the mothers.

To the mothers, therefore, I would again and again address the request to let themselves be governed by their maternal feelings, enlightened by thought, in guiding those rising impressions, in developing that tender germ in the infant's heart. They will find that at first it is yet involved in the animal nature of the infant; that it is an innate feeling, strong, because not yet under the control of reason, and filling the whole mind because not yet opposed by the impulse of conflicting passions. That feeling, let them believe, has been implanted by the Creator. But together with it there exists in the infant that instinctive impulse of its animal nature which is first made subservient to self-preservation and directed towards the satisfaction of natural and necessary wants; which is next bent on gratification, and unless it be checked in time, runs out into a thousand imaginary and artificial wants, hurrying us from enjoyment to enjoyment, and ending in consummate selfishness.

To control and to break this selfish impulse, the best, the only course is for the mother to strengthen daily that better impulse which so soon gives her the pledge by the first smile on the lips, the first glance of affection in the eye of the infant, that though the powers of the intellect are yet slumbering, she may soon speak a language intelligible to the *heart*. She will be enabled by affection and by firmness to bring her child to give up those cravings which render it so unamiable, and to give them up for her, the mother's sake. By what means she can make herself understood— how she can supply the want of words and of precepts—I shall not undertake to answer for her: but let a mother answer whether, conscious as she is of her own love for her child, a love enhanced by reflection, she will not without either words or precepts be able to find the way to the heart and the affection of her infant.

But if the mother has succeeded in this, let her not fancy that she has done everything. The time will come when the hitherto speechless emotions of the infant will find a language—when his eye will wander from the mother to other individuals within the sphere that surrounds him— and when that sphere itself will be extended. His affections must then no longer rest concentrated in one object, and that object though the dearest and kindest of mortals yet a mortal, and liable to those imperfections which "our flesh is heir to." The affections of the child are claimed by higher objects—and indeed by the highest.

Maternal love is the first agent in education; but maternal love though the purest of human feelings is human; and salvation is not of the power of man but of the power of God. Let not the mother fancy that she of her own power and with her best intentions can raise the child's heart and mind beyond the sphere of earthly and perishable things. It is not for her to presume that her instructions or her example will benefit the child, unless they be calculated to lead the child to that faith and to that love from which alone salvation springs.

The love and confidence of the infant in the mother is

but the adumbration of a purer—of the purest and highest feeling which can take up its abode in a mortal breast— of a feeling of love and faith, now no more confined to an individual—now no more mixed with "baser matter"—but rising superior to all other emotions, and *elevating* man by teaching him *humility,* the feeling of love and faith in his Creator and his Redeemer.

In this spirit let education be considered in all its stages; let the physical faculties be developed, but without forgetting that they form the lower series of human nature; let the intellect be enlightened, but let it be remembered that the first science which thought and knowledge should teach is modesty and moderation; let the discipline be regulated and the heart be formed, not by coercion but by sympathy— not by precept but by practice; and above all let it be prepared for that influence from above which alone can restore the image of God in man.

X

THE SWAN SONG

AFTER a period of lingering decline the school at Yverdon was finally closed in 1825. Pestalozzi returned to Neuhof where he engaged actively in literary work and in plans for the establishment of an institution which would serve to insure the continuance of the various educational activities in which he had been engaged. In 1826 he published *The Swan Song,* a final attempt at an exhaustive review of his life's work in the theory and practice of education. The work, much of which had been written at an earlier date, falls into three parts: (1) a discussion of the nature and aim of true elementary education as he had conceived it; (2) an account of his various attempts to apply his educational views in practice; and (3) explanations as to why he had accomplished so little toward the attainment of his aim.

Notwithstanding rather frequent repetitions and an increased prolixity of style the work ranks among the most important of Pestalozzi's educational writings.

The Swan Song

Seyffarth, 12, 293–398

The idea of elementary training, in the theoretical and practical exposition of which I have spent the greater part of my later years is nothing else than the idea of conformity to nature in the unfolding and development of the capacities and powers of the human race.

But in order to approach even distantly to this conformity to nature one must ask himself— What is human nature? What is the essence, what are the distinctive characteristics of human nature as such? It cannot well be the capacities and powers which man shares in common with the lower animals. It must, then, be the capacities and powers which distinguish man from the non-human animals which constitute what is essentially human in man. It is not my body nor my bodily appetites but the capacities of my human heart and my human intellect and my artistic powers which constitute my human nature. From which it naturally follows that the problem of elementary education is simply that of the development, in conformity with nature, of the capacities and powers of the human mind and heart and hand. The conformity to nature implied in the idea of elementary education requires, then, the subordination of our animal nature to the higher demands of our higher powers. It follows, further, that the means employed in promoting the development of our powers and capacities presuppose, if not a clear knowledge, at least a lively inner feeling of the course of nature in the unfolding and upbuilding of our powers and capacities. This course rests upon eternal, unchanging laws which in the case of every individual human power are bound up with an irresistible impulse toward its development.

The natural course of our development has its origin in these impulses. Man wills to do everything for which he feels that he possesses the requisite powers and it is these

impulses which impel him to this. The feeling of this power
is an expression of the eternal, indestructible, unchanging
laws which lie back of the course of nature in the development of our capacities.

These laws, which are a product of the peculiar quality
of every individual human capacity, differ among themselves as do the powers within which they dwell; but they
all arise, as do these powers, from the unity of human nature and hence with all their differences they are all related
to each other, and it is only through the harmony and balance in which they exist side by side in our race that they
conform to nature and exercise an educational influence.
It is a truth which holds good in all cases that only that
which affects man in the totality of his nature, that is, in
heart, mind and hand, only that is for him really, truly
and naturally educative. Everything which fails to impress,
in this way, man's nature in its totality fails to conform to
nature and to exercise a truly educative influence. Whatever makes upon him a one-sided impression, whether it
be upon the heart, the mind or hand, undermines and destroys the balance of our powers, violates nature and contributes to the mis-education of our race. It is eternally true
that the means which are peculiarly adapted to arouse the
feelings of my heart do not educate the human intellect,
nor can, on the other hand, the means by which the human
intellect is naturally developed contribute to ennoble naturally and effectively the human heart.

Every one-sided development of our powers is untrue and
unnatural, it is only sham education, it is the sounding
brass and tinkling cymbal of human education and not
human education itself.

THE SWAN SONG

True and natural education from its very nature leads to a striving toward perfection, to a striving toward a rounding out of our human powers. One-sidedness of education leads from its very nature to the undermining, and the dissolution of that general power of human nature out of which this striving truly and naturally issues.

The unity of our natural powers is a divine gift to our race for our ennoblement and in this respect also it is eternally true— What God hath joined together let no man put asunder. If he does this in regard to any feature of our education, whatever, he makes half-men of us for whom no help is to be either sought or found.

Every one-sided excess in the training of our powers leads to the self-deception of baseless pretensions, to misjudgment of our weaknesses and defects and to a harsh judgment of all those who do not assent to the erroneous views which our one-sidedness has led us to entertain. . . .

That is just as true of men who go to extremes in the cultivation of their emotional and religious natures as it is of those who in the pursuit of selfish ends commit a similar error in regard to their purely intellectual powers.

All one-sided over-development of a single faculty leads to an exaggeration (*Aufgedunsenheit*) of its claims which in its inmost essence is lame and dead.

That is just as true of love and faith as it is of the intellect or of the professional and artistic skill of our race.

The inner foundations of domestic and civil welfare are essentially spiritual in character and the practical skill, which domestic and civil life also require, is, without these, dangerously deceptive and the source of confusion, discontent, and offense in both domestic and civil life.

The harmonious development of the faculties so essential to the idea of elementary education requires the natural development of every one of the fundamental human powers. Each one of these unfolds in accordance with eternal, unchanging laws and its development is natural only in so far as it is in harmony with these laws. Every infraction of these laws makes the course of development unnatural. The laws which underlie the natural development of each one of our faculties are in themselves essentially different. The human intellect does not develop in accordance with the same laws as those according to which our emotional nature develops. And those, according to which our senses and limbs develop, differ from both of these.

But every individual faculty is developed simply through use.

Man develops naturally the fundamental virtues of love and faith only through the exercise of love and faith. Again, man's powers of thought are developed only through training. Skill in the arts and crafts, in the use of the senses and of the limbs is developed only through practice.

Moreover, man is impelled by the very nature of every one of these powers to use it. The eye *will* see, the ear *will* hear, the foot *will* walk, the hand *will* grasp. And so also with the heart. It *will* love and trust. The mind *will* think.

There lies in every one of our faculties, physical and mental, an impulse to rise out of a condition of inertness and impotence into one of trained efficiency.

But just as, in the case of a child that is learning to walk, its desire to walk is momentarily checked if, at its first attempt, it falls and hurts itself, so its faith and trust is checked if the cat to which it stretches out its hand scratches it, or the dog which it strokes, barks and shows its teeth.

Again, the child's impulse to develop its reasoning powers through use is checked if the means by which one is trying to teach it to think do not attract and stimulate the intellect, but rather burden and confuse it. The course of nature in the development of our powers, if left to itself makes slow progress in rising above the sensual and the animal in our race, and is hampered by these. If it is to achieve the development of the human in man it must rely, on the one hand, on the assistance of the enlightened love, which arises from the father-, mother-, brother-, sister-instinct in our nature; and, on the other, on the enlightened use of the art of education which is the product of thousands of years of human effort.

Thus the idea of elementary education, more accurately defined, is nothing else than the result of the efforts of the human race to supplement the course of nature in the development of our powers with all that the enlightened love, the trained understanding and the intelligent artistry of our race can provide.

However sacred and divine the course of nature may be as fundamental to the development of our race, nevertheless, when left entirely to itself, it is actuated only by animal instincts. To inspire it with human and divine motives is the duty of our race, and the aim of the idea of elementary education, as well as that of wisdom and piety.

If we take a closer look at this position from the moral, intellectual, domestic and civic standpoint, and ask ourselves: How does the foundation of our moral life, love and faith, actually, truly and naturally develop in our race, and how may the earliest germs of our moral and religious

life be nourished, vitalized and strengthened by human care
and skill? If we do this we shall find that it is the quiet
and secure enjoyment of the satisfaction of his physical
needs which vitalizes and develops the moral powers of the
infant from birth on. . . .

It is the sacred mother love, it is the instinct-like attention to the satisfaction of every need of the child which we
must recognize as that which engenders in the child the
feeling of trust in, and love for the source of this satisfaction; and it is through fostering the growth of this love
and trust that moral and religious character is developed.

Hence it is the maintenance of the infant in a condition
of quietude and contentment and the utilization of this for
awakening in the child those feelings that distinguish man
from all other creatures, which is of the higher importance
in the education of our race.

Every disquietude, which disturbs, at this period, the
vegetating life of child, lays the foundation for vitalizing
and strengthening the incitements and demands of our
sensual-animal nature, and for weakening the development
of those powers and capacities which constitute the essence
of humanity.

The first and most effective provision for the maintenance of this condition of peaceful calm during the earliest
period of childhood is made by nature in the heart of the
mother. It manifests itself in our race in general in the
strength and loyalty of motherhood. The lack of this
strength and loyalty is the characteristic of the unnatural
mother. . . .

Let the cause be what it may, where the child lacks the
tender hand and the smiling eye of the mother, he lacks

himself the smile and the good humor that is characteristic of the child under normal conditions. . . .

On the other hand an excess of sensual gratification undermines that condition of peacefulness in which the germs of love and trust naturally unfold. . . .

The moderation naturally characteristic of the mother is not calculated to excite sensuality but only to satisfy the child's physical wants.

The natural moderation of motherly care, although instinctive, is yet quite in harmony with the demands of the mind and the heart. It has its foundation in the mind and in the heart and owes only its stimulation to instinct, hence it is not a consequence of the subjection of the higher and nobler faculties to the sensual desires of the flesh.

It is along this road that the influence of the mother develops naturally in the infant the earliest traces of love and of faith and at the same time tends to disseminate these throughout the whole family circle. The instinctive love and faith of the child for the mother is raised in this way to a human love and faith. The child's circle of human love and trust tends continually to extend itself outward. Whom the mother loves, the child loves. Whom the mother trusts the child trusts. Even when the mother says of a strange man whom the child has not previously seen: "He loves you, you must trust him, he is a good man, give him your little hand," the child smiles and gives him its hand. Or again, if she says to him, "You have a grandfather far away who loves you," the child believes in his love. And in the same way if she says to him, "I have a Father in heaven from Whom comes everything that we have," the child believes what she says. . . . And so the child is naturally led from a lower to a higher form of love and faith. And this is the road along which the idea of elementary education seeks to work toward the establishment of the religious and moral life of the child.

I proceed further and enquire:

How do the foundations of the intellectual life of man naturally develop in our race, his ability to think, to reflect, to investigate and to judge? We find that the education of our powers of thought originates in the impression which the perception of all objects makes upon us, since they affect both our inner and outer sense and arouse the intellect's indwelling impulse to develop itself.

The perception, heightened by this impulse leads above all to a consciousness of the impression which the objects have made upon us and at the same time to a knowledge of these. This produces necessarily a feeling of the need of giving expression to the impressions which our perception has made upon us, and above all the feeling of the need of imitating it, at the same time also, and much more humanly, the feeling of the need of the power of speech, the development of which will make imitation superfluous.

This faculty of speech, essential to the development of our thinking powers, is to be considered chiefly as a faculty of service to human nature in making fruitful and general the knowledge acquired through observation. It develops naturally from the beginning only in close connection with the growth of the knowledge derived from the senses and the latter usually precedes it. The human race can naturally talk about nothing which it has not known. It cannot speak of anything in any other manner than that according to which it learned it. What it has learned erroneously, it speaks of erroneously, and what in this case was true from the beginning is true yet. . . .

The natural method of learning the mother tongue or any other language is connected with the knowledge acquired through observation and the natural procedure in the learning of both must be in harmony with the course of nature according to which the impressions derived from observation pass over into knowledge. If we fix this point of view in mind so far as it concerns the learning of the mother tongue we find: That just as everything distinctively and essentially human develops only slowly and step by step from our animal nature so the ability to speak the mother tongue, both as regards the organs of speech and as regards the knowledge of the language itself, develops slowly step by step. The child cannot speak so long as his speech organs are undeveloped. At the beginning, however, it knows practically nothing and hence can have no desire to speak of anything. The child's will and ability to speak develop only in proportion to the knowledge which it gradually acquires through experience.

Nature knows no other way of teaching the infant to speak, and art in assisting to this end must pursue the same slow method. But it must seek to promote the process by applying all the stimuli, which the different objects in the child's environment and the variety of tones of the organs of speech can afford.

In order to teach the child to speak the mother must make nature itself work upon the child inciting him to see, hear, feel, etc. Just as the consciousness of what it sees, hears, feels, and tastes is vivified, so its will to know and to use expressions for these impressions, that is, its will to learn to speak, is strengthened. To this end the mother must use also the incitement of tone.

In so far as the mother wishes to hasten the attainment by her child of the ability to speak she must bring the various tones to his attention, pronouncing them now loudly, now gently, sometimes singing and sometimes laughing, so that the child will feel a desire to imitate her; and she must likewise accompany her words with the impression of the objects, the names of which she wishes the child to learn. She must present these objects to its senses in their most important relationships and in the most various and stimulating positions, and must keep them before him and proceed in the training in expression only in proportion as the child's impressions have become mature. The art, or rather, the enlightened care of the mother can accelerate and enliven the course of nature in learning to speak and one of the tasks of elementary education is to investigate the means of accomplishing this end and to present to mothers a clear, definite and properly arranged series of exercises adapted to attain this end. . . .

The learning of any other language takes place more rapidly. The child who learns a foreign language, whether ancient or modern, has (1) already trained organs of speech. In the case of every foreign language it has to learn only the few tones peculiar to this language. (2) By the time a child takes up a foreign language it knows millions of things which it can express with the greatest definiteness.

Therefore the learning of every new language is essentially nothing else than learning to change tones, the meaning of which in the mother tongue is known to him, into tones which are not known. The art of facilitating this

228

change through mnemonic means and of arranging in psychological order series of exercises which will naturally clarify the ideas, verbal knowledge of which was to be facilitated, is again to be considered as one of the most essential of the tasks of the science of elementary education. The need of a psychological foundation for the initial stages of language instruction is generally recognized, and I believe that through my experiments, inaugurated a half-century ago and carried on uninterruptedly ever since, for the simplification of the early steps in education, I believe that through these I have discovered some natural and effective means of attaining this end.

In order, however, not to lose the thread of my exposition of the idea of elementary education I must revert to the thesis that an intellectual education based upon direct experience must rely largely upon a natural method of language teaching. This aid is an outgrowth of sense perception and contributes to the clarification of knowledge. The nature of intellectual education is such, however, as to require broader foundations than this. It requires a method of developing the child's ability to classify and compare the objects which it has clearly apprehended. In this way its capacity for judging correctly of these objects and their qualities will develop into real intellectual ability. . . .

Intellectual development, and the race culture which depends on this, demand the continual development of the logical means for the natural development of the powers of thought, investigation and judgment, to the conscious use of which man attained thousands of years ago. These means are, in their character and scope, an outgrowth of our ability freely and independently to group together, to

separate and to compare the objects which we have learned
to know through direct observation, in other words, they
are an outgrowth of our power of logically conceiving and
dealing with material and of attaining in this way to cultivated judgment.

The investigation of these means of raising the thinking
capacity of our race to a cultivated judgment, their improvement and the making them available for general use, are,
again, essential aims of the idea of elementary education.
And, since the power of working over logically the material acquired through the senses is plainly first stimulated
and exercised in counting and measuring, it is evident that
the most effective means of attaining this important end is
to be sought and found in a simplified elementary arithmetic and geometry. And this shows why the idea of elementary education recognizes and adopts the psychologically
organized and simplified study of form and number, combined with a likewise simplified study of speech as constituting together the profoundest and most effective
general foundation of a method of developing the thinking
powers. . . .

If, thirdly, we ask ourselves: How are the foundations of
the art developed, out of which are produced the means of
giving outer expression to the products of the human mind,
and of giving effect to the impulses of the human heart,
and by which all the forms of skill required in domestic
and civil life must be developed? If we ask this question,
we see at once that these foundations are both internal and
external, they are mental and physical; but we also see that
all cultivation of skill in the arts and crafts consists essentially in the training of intellectual power, in training of

the powers of perception. We cannot avoid the conclusion that he who has been naturally and adequately trained in the elements of reckoning, of measuring, and of the related art of drawing has already acquired the essential fundamentals of all art and artistic skill, and that he needs only to bring the external powers of his senses and his limbs into harmony with this internally developed skill in the particular art which he wishes to acquire.

Just as the elementary number and form study must be considered as the peculiar gymnastic of the mental factors of artistic skill so the mechanical exercises of the senses and the hand, which are necessary to the training of the external factors of artistic skill, are to be recognized as the physical gymnastic.

The elementary training of artistic skill, of which vocational training must be considered only as a special adaptation to the social rank and to the relationships peculiar to each individual, depends, therefore, upon two different foundations. The natural means of cultivating it consists in the stimulation and training of two different fundamental powers, mental and physical. These become, however, means for genuine, human education only through the training in common of the three fundamental capacities of the race, or, what amounts to the same thing, through the training of that in our nature which is peculiar to man.

I have touched upon what is essential in the elementary training of these means in their moral and intellectual foundations, I now turn to the physical. As the stimulus to the education of our moral and intellectual capacities lies in their natural impulse to develop themselves, so the stimuli to the natural development of the physical factors of artistic skill are to be found in the natural tendencies of these toward self development. The urge toward activity exists in our organs of sense and in our limbs, and, mentally and physically stimulated, renders practically inevitable the inclination to make use of these powers. As far as stimulation is concerned, the art has little to do. The physical impulse to use the senses and the limbs is aroused, essentially, by our animal instincts. The subordination of this instinctive stimulation to the laws of the moral and intellectual foundations of the art is what our earliest efforts toward a natural development of our capacity has to accomplish. In this they will find powerful support in the circumstances and relationships of each individual and in the concentrated moral, intellectual and physical influences of domestic life. The wise and careful use of the means of education afforded by domestic life is just as important in physical education as it is in moral or intellectual. The inequality of these means is determined by the difference in the circumstances and relationships of home life in which each individual finds himself. But in the midst of the confusion arising from the difference in the means of education for the utilization of the fundamental powers of our nature, the essential feature of the development of these means, physical as well as moral and intellectual, is everywhere subordinated to eternal, unchanging laws.

. . . Before proceeding farther, I shall face the question, "Is not the idea of elementary education a dream, is it the basis of a really practicable procedure?" From many sides I hear the question, "Where is this education actually carried out?"

I answer, everywhere and nowhere. Everywhere you can find proofs of the practicability of certain features of it, nowhere is it carried out in its entirety. As a single method, adopted as a whole, demonstrating systematically the different means employed, it exists nowhere. Nowhere does there exist a completely organized elementary school. The knowledge and the practical ability of our race, in all fields, is a patchwork, and what is highest and best in our civilization is developed and organized only piece by piece. As regards every single feature of unevenly developing civilization man sometimes advances and sometimes recedes. No situation ever will or can arise in which the demands of this great idea will ever be met to general satisfaction. Human nature places insuperable obstacles in the way of a general and complete carrying out of this idea and the human weakness of our minds and our hearts, whose divine inner nature is enclosed in this garment of flesh and blood, never permits our race to attain perfection in regard to any feature of its development. . . .

Even the most powerful must, as regards every attempt of his at self-development, say with Paul, "Not that I have attained, but that I strive that I may attain." And if this is true as regards individual, it is infinitely truer as regards all the collective efforts of our race toward culture. No institution, even though it be equipped in princely fashion with moral and intellectual aids, can ever succeed in introducing and securing recognition for the idea of elementary education as a perfect method of instruction and education for all classes.

I repeat human nature is irresistibly opposed to the complete and general introduction of this lofty idea. All of our knowledge and ability is a patchwork and will continue to be a patchwork to the end of time, and every advance in knowledge, ability, and even in will power proceeding, as it does, from the limited advances of individual men and of individual groups, will always continue to be a patchwork of our knowledge and ability. Moreover, it will always place hindrances in the path of the progressive individual who seeks to complete this patchwork.

We must say it, a method of instruction and of education entirely adequate to the requirements of the idea of elementary education is unthinkable.

However clearly its principles may be stated, however much its means may be simplified, however clear the inner harmony of its execution may be made, no external harmony of the means of carrying it out is thinkable; every individual man, according to the peculiarities of his individuality will carry it out differently from every other. One will find in his heart the strength with which to strive toward carrying the idea into practice; another will find it in his intellectual superiority and seek to find the way toward the attainment of his goal in the clearness and correctness of his ideas. Again, another will seek it in his superior artistic skill and vocational efficiency; and it is really good that such is the case. There are geniuses of the heart, geniuses of the intellect and of artistic and practical skill. God has created them. To some He has given a million-fold, but one-sided advantage over their fellowmen. They are millionaires so far as the moral, intellectual and physical powers of our race are concerned, but are inspired in their feeling, thinking and acting by selfishness, as we have occasion to notice every day in the money-and-power-millionaires in our midst. Like the money-millionaires they have a string of dependents who, in the interest of the maintenance of the claims of the particular powers in which they excel, combat the claims of the opposing powers. The result of this must necessarily be that every excess of some particular power contributes to the maintenance of the equilibrium of all. It contributes also to the maintenance of the piecemeal type of progress by which human nature advances.

We must recognize that all progress is knowledge and skill is naturally of this piecemeal character and that with this is connected the reality of the benefit which we derive from such progress.

So long as we do not recognize this, we must acknowledge that the idea of elementary education is merely a delusive dream and that the carrying out of the idea, in such a manner as to attain all its aims, is impossible. As soon, however, as we recognize the aim of elementary education as the aim of all human culture, and the naturalness of the progress of all our knowledge as consisting in its patchwork character, which generally sets a definite limit to our knowledge and practical capacity, we come to see that the aim of this great idea is identical with the aim of the human race. This disposes of the statement, that we in our blindness make, namely, that it is an empty dream and in itself incapable of being carried out.

No, whatever may be the goal of the race, the effort to attain it is my duty. The duty of the race can never be impracticable nor unattainable and must never be considered as such. And that is truly the case with the idea of elementary education when it is rightly conceived. Just as it is

undeniably true that, as a method, it will never attain the
goal of inner completion, so, it is no less certain, that it lies
in the nature of the simple, natural, unsophisticated man
to strive for it, and that we have to thank this urge, found
generally in human nature, for the degree of moral, intellectual and physical culture which the civilized world has
attained. Every principle of a natural education, every natural means employed in any subject of instruction whatever, is its work.

Once more I say, this lofty idea is everywhere and nowhere. Just as in its perfected form it is nowhere, so in
partial revelations and in intermittent efforts it is seen
everywhere. To ignore it is to ignore everything that is
divine and everlasting in human nature. This divine and
eternal is in its essence human nature itself. It is, in its
essence, the only feature of our nature that is truly human,
and the naturalness of the means of education which the
idea of elementary education requires, is, essentially, nothing other than the harmony of this means with that divine
spark within us, which is eternally in conflict with our
sensual, animal nature. Sensual self-seeking is the very
essence of the animal nature and whatever is produced from
it and is actuated by its charm, is, when conceived in a
purely human way, unnatural.

Hence the demands of the idea of elementary education
are nothing other than the demands of true conformity to
our higher nature, and are in eternal conflict with artifice
and with the sensual dominance of the unnatural, which
arises from the sway of the flesh over the spirit. The general
opinion of those who pay excessive attention to the education of the people rather than to that of the individual, is

opposed to the consideration of the claims of elementary education and to the influence of natural means which it employs. It could not be otherwise. The provision for the education of a people demands energy, skill and effort of a physical rather than of a moral and intellectual character. The flesh in all its shapes and forms is to be subordinated to the spirit and the idea of elementary education leads to an earnest and active recognition of the need of this subordination.

When I consider the entire scope of my efforts to gain recognition for the idea of elementary education, I cannot conceal from myself a feeling of the inexpressible need of it in the beginnings of folk education for all classes.

This powerfully inspired me to unceasing efforts to simplify the usual forms of popular instruction as the best and most certain means of remedying the evil. But in me this lofty idea was the product of a kindly, loving heart, combined with a disproportionate weakness of the mental and practical power which might have given the strivings of my heart an important influence on the actual promotion of this lofty purpose. It was, in me, the product of an extremely active imagination, which could accomplish nothing, restricted as it was by the routine of the life of the time. On the contrary, it made me seem like a child engaged in a contest with powerful men who opposed his visionary aspirations. Under these circumstances my efforts could accomplish no result of any greater importance than the, in part, vivid and brilliant but, in general, ineffective stimulation of others, which they actually brought about. The natural means of education of our race which are spiritual in character appeal, on the other hand, to the individual in whom the spiritual predominates. They must appeal to him in this proportion.

While the unnatural artificiality of worldliness, sensual gratification, the impulse to imitation, and the powerful influence of the crowd, influence the animal nature of our race, the naturalness of the Elementary Method and of the means it employs, appeals to the spiritually minded even in cases where their beneficent influence has not been previously felt. It increases the receptivity to moral and intellectual stimuli and also the innocence and self-forgetfulness which give rise to this receptivity. In this way the Elementary Method is also fitted to counteract successfully the attractions and the consequences of what is unnatural in the means employed for the education and the stimulation of our race.

The experience of the entire cultural life of our race bears witness, in all epochs of its history, to the attractive influence of naturalness in the means employed for the development of our powers. Exactly the same thing is claimed for the idea of elementary education wherever it comes into contact with simple and natural human beings. But one must not seek it in a dream of the possibility of its universal and complete realization, but rather in the partial representations of it everywhere stimulated, but everywhere incomplete, ever striving toward perfection and approaching it. And so it appears to the investigator in a thousand forms attractive and interesting as the innocence and purity of the human heart.

I now turn to the consideration, from the moral, intellectual and physical point of view, of the result of our attempts to investigate the effect of the elementary method upon the education of humanity in its relation to the great fundamental principle, "It is life that educates."

As regards moral education, the Elementary Method connects with the life of the child in that it is based upon the instinctive love of the parents and of brothers and sisters. It is undeniable that the faith and love, which we regard as the God-given beginning-points of morality and religiosity, are to be sought in the father- and mother-love of the home, consequently in the actual life of the child.

Our institution cannot claim to have had experience in this matter with children from the cradle up. But it is none the less certain that the Elementary Method, on account of its simplicity, is adapted for use in moral education from the cradle up, and, indeed, much earlier, and more effectively than in intellectual or art education. The child trusts and loves before it thinks and acts, and the influence of home life stimulates in it the development of the moral powers on which all human thought and action depend. In spite of our lack of experience with children in the cradle, our experiments enable us to say this. The simplicity of the means of elementary education, which makes every child capable of practising or of communicating to other children what he sees and knows, has given us abundant evidence of its moral influence. In our school family the stimulation of brotherly and sisterly feeling and the resulting mutual love and confidence has at different periods in the history of our institution achieved results which have convinced many noble souls that our work is adapted to build up and strengthen the influence of home life on moral development, and to bring it into harmony with the course of nature to a degree which is urgently needed in these degenerate times, but which is very difficult to attain.

As regards intellectual education the Elementary Method is in accordance with the principle, "It is life that educates." Just as moral education proceeds essentially from the internal observation of ourselves, that is, from impressions which appeal to our inner nature; so intellectual education proceeds from the observation of objects which appeal to and stimulate our external senses. Nature connects all our sense impressions with our life. All our knowledge of the outer world is the result of our sense impressions of the same. Even our dreams originate from these. The impulse toward self-development, which exists in all our faculties, leads us involuntarily to exercise our senses and our limbs and to see, hear, taste, smell, feel, grasp, walk, etc. But our hearing, smelling, tasting, feeling, walking, grasping is educative only in so far as it develops the power of the eye to see clearly, that of the ear to hear clearly, etc. This education to right hearing, seeing, feeling, etc., depends upon the completion, the maturing of the impressions which the perceived objects have made upon our senses. Wherever the impression made by an act of perception is not completed, not matured in our senses then we do not know the object in all its details. We know it only superficially. The knowledge of it is not educative. It does not affect the impulse toward development. Its results do not satisfy our nature and whatever is not satisfying to human nature is not based upon a natural foundation.

Just as moral education has in instinctive parental love a divinely given middle point for its natural development, so intellectual education must proceed from a central point which is adapted to bring the perception, which we derive from the senses, to a completeness which satisfies our nature. Only thus can it become educative and natural.

If we now enquire, where is this middle point in which the sensory elements of our intellectual education are united? we find it nowhere else than in the home circle which the child, from the cradle on, is accustomed to observe from morning to night. It is undoubtedly the repetition of the observation of objects, it is the frequent and varied appearance of these objects before the child's senses, which brings to completion and maturity the impression they make upon him. It is also true that the living-rooms of the men who have a living-room is the central point, and that, in general, there is no place outside the home circle in which the objects for observation by the child from the cradle on appear before his senses so continuously, so uninterruptedly, so variously, and in a manner so attractive to human nature. It is in this circle that the need is felt of distinguishing between the means of developing the human powers, and the training in the knowledge and skill which every child needs individually according to his station in life and his circumstances. And here again, the special technical skill which the child individually needs is associated with the developed fundamental powers out of which the special training must naturally arise.

And since the former, the means of developing, general human capacity, are, and must be, in all classes, and in all relationships essentially the same while, on the contrary, the means of cultivating special vocational skill are essentially different, the principle "It is life that educates" must in this regard be considered from two different points of view. In the first place the question arises "How is the influence of life adapted to develop naturally the powers of human nature?" and, secondly, "To what extent is this influence adapted to cultivate skill in the special, vocational applications of the developed general capacities of the child?" The answer is simple. It develops the general human powers even under the most widely different circumstances according to eternal unchanging laws, which in their natural influence upon the child are the same, whether he creeps in the dust or is heir to a throne. As regards the special application of these powers, life works upon each individual, whom it educates, in complete harmony with the difference in circumstances, station in life and relationships in which the child that is to be educated, finds itself, and also in harmony with the peculiarity of the capacities and talents of the individual child. Hence this last influence is extremely varied.

From this is to be inferred what assistance the art of the Elementary Method may afford to the natural unfolding of the child's powers of observation. And that is nothing else than to bring the objects in the child's home surroundings before his senses in an attractive and impressive manner and thus cause them to exercise upon him an influence that is, in the true sense of the word, educational. This shows that the elementary means of educating the powers of observation are fundamentally nothing else than the psychological means of stimulating the impulse to activity which lies within these powers. They are simply the results of human effort to make the impressions derived from the objects of observation educative for the child through making them more enduring and stimulating.

I proceed further. The elementary art of educating the powers of observation, by its very nature, calls forth the natural development of the powers of speech, that is, the educatively stimulated impressions received from objects, by their very nature, call forth man's power of expressing himself.

The natural cultivation of this faculty, is naturally connected with the course of nature in the development of the powers of observation. The education of the powers of speech like that of the perceptive powers is a product of life itself. The principle "It is life that educates," is just as true of the education of the powers of speech as it is of that of the powers of observation. It is undeniable that the course of nature in the development of the latter, as of the former, is from life outward, and the education of these powers is natural only in so far as it follows this course, that is, only so far as it is in harmony with this great, universal, divinely ordained fundamental principle of human education. And it is equally certain that this harmony can be brought about only through connecting all means employed with the home life, and, in consequence, with the entire circle of knowledge of this life. This knowledge in the form of definite ideas should already be in the child's mind before one presents to him the arbitrary word symbols by which these are so differently expressed in different languages.

When one begins to place in the mouth of the child empty words as if these constituted real knowledge or the means of acquiring real knowledge he deviates from the principle, "It is life that educates," and, when he does this, he implants in the child the root of all that is perverted and unnatural in the use of the divine gift of speech. In so doing he lays the foundation for arrogance and harshness and, thereby, the foundation of the greatest evil of our time, for the artificiality which results from the superficiality of all knowledge and from the falsity of our speech. This leads our race to mire in the bog of error and arrogance and selfishness, which is characteristic of the superficiality of human knowledge in all forms and relationships. The manifold consequences of this our age knows to its sorrow.

The characteristic of the method of language instruction which is derived from the observance of the principle, "It is life that educates," is, that it creates for the knowledge derived from experience a higher degree of usefulness. The method proceeds from the naming of objects to that of qualities and actions, that is, to the adjectives and verbs which express these qualities, and actions. The more extended and definite the child's sensory knowledge of objects, their qualities and actions, the more extended and definite are the natural foundations of language instruction. The more limited and indefinite the child's knowledge of these objects and qualities, the more limited and confused are the genuine and solid foundations of language instruction. Thus language instruction for every individual child is dependent upon the extent and definiteness of his sensory knowledge, and the language teacher, if he finds the pupil deficient in this knowledge, must seek to remedy this deficiency before he proceeds further with language instruction.

The natural rate of progress in learning to speak, that is,

in learning the mother tongue, can, then, in no case be more rapid, or more educative, than the child's progress in sensory knowledge. So that, if a child requires many years to acquire a clear and accurate knowledge of the objects in his environment he will require many years, also, to learn to express himself clearly in regard to them. He can proceed naturally in learning only in proportion as his impressions of the objects, derived from direct observation, become more vivid and definite. The art of promoting the natural development of the child's powers of expression is helped forward in proportion as his sense-impressions are varied and definite. The art of naturally extending and vivifying the impressions received from without is the only true basis for any method of facilitating the learning of the mother tongue. The externals of speech, the tones themselves, unless they are vitally related to the impressions which give them meaning are vain and empty. They become parts of human speech only through consciousness of their relationship to the sense-impressions. At first, the training of the child's powers of speech through what he hears others say, is for a long time merely mechanical; but this mechanical preparation for speech demands the entire attention of those who exercise an influence upon the child's learning to speak. The words, which the infant hears those about him speak, come only gradually to have an intellectually educative influence upon him. For a long time they make on him only a merely sensory impression like the sound of a bell, or a hammer or any of the sounds of nature. But for method of teaching language this impression is important. The sound impression, as such, becomes more and more accurate. As it becomes more and more accurate it passes over gradually into the power to reproduce the sound. At this age the child learns to pronounce a number of word sounds without knowing their meaning; but this prepares it for grasping the meaning more readily and retaining much better than if he had not already become familiar with its sound and its pronunciation.

But the Elementary Method does not content itself merely with the impressions which nature presents accidentally and confusedly to the child's senses, with using these impressions, just as they happen to come, for the education of his powers of speech. It extends its influence to arranging these in accordance with the actual needs of human nature, and with bringing their use into harmony with these needs. . . .

It must do so, for it is noteworthy that just as it is necessary and good for the development of the child's perceptive powers that the number of objects of observation in his surroundings should be sufficiently comprehensive for the development in him of the knowledge that he really needs, but should not so exceed the requirements of his station in life, his relationships and abilities that it should exercise a paralyzing, weakening and confusing influence upon his knowledge, so it is equally necessary that the vocabulary, within the limits of which the child should learn to speak, should be comprehensive enough for the needs of his station in life, his relationships and capacities but should not exceed these limits to such an extent as to exert upon him a weakening and distracting influence.

This point of view is equally true and important as regards the means of development of all human powers. Even the poorest, even the child in the most meagre circumstances can never, so far as his fundamental powers are concerned, receive too much of an elementary education if it is conducted in conformity to nature. One cannot go too far in attempting through a natural elementary system of education to cultivate kindness, intelligence and habits of industry; but the education in the practical application of these must always be limited by his actual circumstances. And it is here that the Elementary Method is peculiarly adapted to test the child's knowledge of things and of speech through the means employed in acquiring it. Educational procedure must always, in the case of every individual child, be considered as in the service of actual life. Education even in the first stages of the child's training must never, in promoting the development of his powers of speech and of observation, lead to the acquisition of a knowledge of speech or of things that would work to the disadvantage of the needs of actual life. He must never acquire that knowledge which is not only not applicable, but is of such a character as to introduce confusion into his course of training at a time when it is especially important that it should harmonize with actual life.

So important is the recognition of the difference in conformity to nature in the development of human powers and in their practical application. It is remarkable how closely the difference between the means of developing our powers and the means of training to a practical use of them is related to the difference in degree to which those in different ranks of society should be trained in observation, in language, thought and artistic skill. The inner connection of these two differences leads one to see how necessary it is that education in its early stages should adhere closely to the course of nature both in the development of human capacity and in training in the practical application of this capacity. The peace of mankind and the true happiness of all classes depends [sic] upon the general and serious recognition of this truth. Erroneous opinions regarding these principles derived from domestic and public education, threaten to weaken and gradually to dissolve the bonds of social life.

I go farther. Conformity to nature in the learning of any foreign language is quite different from such conformity in learning the mother tongue. The art consists wholly in finding natural means of facilitating the change of sounds of the mother tongue, whose meaning is known, into the sounds of another tongue, which were not heretofore known to the pupil. If the method of making this change is natural, from the psychological and mnemonic point of view, it will be infinitely easy, although differing entirely from the highly artificial routine procedure of the customary method of language instruction. It rests upon the incontrovertible principle: Learning to speak is in itself, at first, not a matter of intellectual training but of hearing others speak and of speaking oneself. The observance of grammatical rules is nothing other than a means of testing whether the natural method of learning to speak and of hearing others speak has attained its end. These rules are formulated at the end of a psychologically well organized process of language learning and not at the beginning.

But in the matter of learning foreign languages, the learning to speak has long been unnaturally separated from language study, the intellectual content of which should be brought before the child in the ordinary use of the language, before it is brought to a clear knowledge of the same through the learning of rules.

This is indeed conceded here and there so far as the modern languages are concerned: it would be impossible to do otherwise. The principle is denied, however, as regards the dead languages. This is due to the fact that instruction in these languages has been brought to a high degree of development notwithstanding the incompleteness and the defects in the routine methods of teaching them to beginners. In its more advanced stages, the teaching of Latin and Greek has been placed upon a sound psychological foundation. However correct this may be, it is nevertheless equally true that the lower stages of instruction in the ancient languages can be considered as in conformity to nature neither in a psychological nor in a mnemonic sense. So positively convinced am I of this that I venture to say definitely that the present routine procedure in the learning of the elements of Latin is psychologically and mnemonically artificial and unnatural. I am quite well aware that such a statement as this by one who is personally acquainted neither with the ancient languages nor with the progress that has been made in teaching them, may seem intolerably and offensively presumptuous. But, if on the one hand, I fully recognize my incompetency to judge the more advanced stages of instruction in the ancient languages, I may, on the other hand, add that just this ignorance of the refinements of the artificial methods of language instruction has aided me in a measure in my efforts, first, to simplify the methods of language instruction and of folk instruction in general, and, secondly, to bring them into harmony with the course of nature and thus to render them psychologically more effective and fruitful. It has enabled me also to investigate more thoroughly the natural procedure in learning the dead languages, than would have been possible had I acquired a complete mastery of the ancient and modern languages in one of the better of their routine forms.

I soon saw that the means of intellectual education derived from the simplified instruction in number and form are weakened in their influence upon education and, in general, are rendered ineffective if they are not associated with a no less thorough simplification of language instruction. And, since I, personally, can make no claim upon the more thorough-going revision of the simplified instruction in number and form but must confess my utter incapacity so far as these two subjects are concerned, nevertheless, I have directed my attention especially to the stage intermediate between the development of the powers of observation and that of thought. And the one contribution which I claim to have made to the improvement of elementary instruction relates solely to the department of language instruction. I have endeavored to acquire the ability to work independently in this field and to make myself master of it through personal research. Hence I have treated it more at length than I have those subjects which I have not investigated and which I do not consider myself capable of investigating.

The natural methods of instruction in every language are the natural means of developing the power of speech and, consequently, they are closely related to the natural methods of developing the perceptive powers. They stand midway between the natural methods of training the powers of observation and those of training the capacity for thought.

The training of the powers of observation, as the basis for the training of the powers of speech is, in combination with the latter, to be considered as the basis for the natural training of the powers of thought. Hence language instruction is essentially the middle stage between the intellectually stimulated perceptive faculty and the faculty of thought.

The methods of training this intermediate faculty are at first essentially mechanical and must be so. The faculty of speech is the organ which utilizes the impressions received through the perceptive powers in the development of the powers of thought.

All three faculties, perception, speech and thought, are to be recognized as the sum total of all means of the development of the intellectual powers. This latter finds in the perceptive faculties the beginning point, in the faculty of speech the middle point, and in the faculty of thought, the conclusion of its natural course of training. The harmony between the methods of cultivating the perceptive powers and those of cultivating the powers of speech strongly confirms this view.

The method of training the perceptive faculty begins with objects, and the recognition of their different qualities and effects constitutes a training for this faculty. Similarly the primary mechanical method of training the faculty of speech begins with the substantives and through the addition to these of adjectives and verbs, which are connected with them in the real world, it becomes a means of passing over from the training of the perceptive powers to that of training the powers of thought.

Just as the great educational principle "It is life that edu-

cates," is true in so far as it applies to the natural development of the perceptive powers so it is no less true and
important as regards the natural development of the faculty
of speech. Indeed it is doubly true in view of the intermediate position which the faculty of speech holds in the
development of faculties of perception and of thought. . . .

These results are determined on the one hand by the
relationship of our inner spiritual nature to the eternal laws
on which our faculty of speech depends. On the other hand,
they are determined also by the million-fold variety of
circumstances, situations, relationships and abilities of the
individuals who are to be educated by them. For this reason
they are in the highest degree, unequal and different.
Hence training in speech, if it is to be given at the time
when the child must learn to speak, is dependent, on the
one hand, on the eternally unchanging laws of the faculty
of speech and, on the other, on the endlessly different conditions and circumstances of the children who are to be
taught.

There is no other natural method of learning to speak
and no other is possible. The way in which man learns to
speak is not an outgrowth of the language method but on
the other hand the language method is a product of man's
capacity for speech. But it is not at all the inequality of external forms of speech, it is the conditions, circumstances
and relationships in which each individual lives; it is the
abilities which each particular individual possesses which
determine just how his powers of speech can be most
naturally developed. It is these facts which in the one case
naturally extend, and, in another case, limit the possibilities
of language attainment.

And what is, in this regard, true in the case of the individual man is also true as regards individual ranks or classes of men. Just as the sensory experiences and the means of using them for purposes of intellectual or esthetic education are more limited in the case of the farmer than in that of the city professional man or merchant, so they are more limited in these latter cases than in that of men of rank or of scholars, or, of those whose wealth frees them from the necessity of sacrificing or restricting themselves for the maintenance of their families.

The glaring differences in the condition of different ranks and classes in regard to the naturalness of the development of their powers of speech reveals the necessity of bringing the method of language instruction into harmony with the conditions of actual life both of individual men and of classes. Only in this way can it achieve recognition as being natural and as being a real boon to the race. The natural methods of developing the powers of speech must, then, as regards their extension or limitation, be organized very differently in each one of the three social classes. In each case they must meet the peculiar needs of the particular class for which they are intended and in no instance must they present any obstacle to the full enjoyment of any benefit that is to be derived. They must, in each of these classes, be connected with the objects, which are morally, intellectually and esthetically necessary to it and which are available for use. Through harmony with these objects, the methods must contribute to their beneficent influence.

. . . I take up the question again and enquire: how does the child learn to speak? How does it prepare itself for speaking from the hour of birth on? And I observe that it is, from this hour on, just as attentive to the tones which sound in its ears as to the objects which are brought to its consciousness through the sense of sight and through every one of its senses.

The development of the organs through which the objects of observation in their entirety are brought to consciousness is intimately connected with the development of the organ through which it learns to speak.

The development of the power of speech must, from the cradle on, proceed step by step with the development of the perceptive faculty. Very early the child feels himself capable of reproducing the tones which it hears and this power, like every other power, is stimulated by the impulse to use and to apply. Through this use the organs of speech are imperceptibly but, from day to day, actually strengthened. Crying, which it does not have to learn, is, in its different articulations, the first expression of its powers of speech. After it come tones which at first have no connection with the articulation of human speech but greatly resemble rather the tones of different kinds of animals. They issue from the urge of the organs, still entirely animal in character, to develop themselves. This impulse is as yet entirely unrelated to the sounds of human speech which the child hears everywhere about him. Only several months later do these tones begin gradually to have a noticeable relation to the sounds of our vowels and consonants and to approximate to the tone of certain syllables and words which are often pronounced before the child. The child now begins to imitate the easiest sounds which the mother pronounces for him. Learning to speak becomes easier and more pleasing to the child day by day and its progress is always combined with that of the child's powers of observation. It proceeds also, step by step, in ever-increasing harmony with the development of the perceptive faculties unless it is diverted from the course of nature by unnatural artifices. And if I now follow this natural order in the learning of the mother tongue, the beginnings of which I have described, I see it continually seeking and finding the course of nature in combining with the development of the perceptive faculties and in using as means of training the life of the home and of the immediate neighborhood.

Thus, as regards the development of the powers of speech, it is life itself which trains man and educates him in a truly natural manner. This development must always progress through the harmonious use of its culture material as a whole. If the education in speech is to be natural, that of the heart, the intellect, and hand must also be natural. To consider these individually and in isolation from each other is to violate the laws which regulate the course of nature.

Such procedure becomes an artificial substitute for the true and reliable means of developing our powers. Children are made to read before they can speak; we try to teach them to speak by the use of books; we turn them away from observation, the natural foundation of speech, and in the most unnatural manner make the dead letter the beginning point for a knowledge of things. Whereas the natural background and beginning point of this knowledge is the thought and life which arises from the observation of nature and these should be recognized as such in all circumstances. Man must be able to speak clearly and correctly about many things before he is mature enough for the intelligent reading of a book. But in our day the appearance of power, rather than the power itself, is what is desired, and all true and reliable means of educating the powers are destroyed by the ever-increasing reliance upon false means of training which are themselves the product of weakness. . . .

And now the method of language instruction or rather the art of learning to speak any language thus conceived becomes quite clear, as I said above. This art is the intermediate stage between the development of the perceptive faculty and that of the faculty of thought. The art of developing the first precedes that of the development of the second. The means of developing the powers of thought has no natural foundation if the natural and adequate development of the powers of observation is lacking.

But what is the natural and sufficiently trained art of observation? When is the art of observation naturally and adequately trained for every class and for every individual?

The answer is clear.

The powers of observation have been sufficiently trained when the ability to observe enables the individual to use freely and confidently his impressions of his surroundings and relationships with clear consciousness as a secure foundation for thought and judgment in regard to these.

This degree of cultivation of the power of observation is, in every case, attainable only in so far as the stage of training intermediate between that of observation and of thought has been brought to the same degree of maturity to which the powers of observation are to be brought if they are to serve as a satisfactorily supplementary basis for the intellectual powers which are to be developed. . . .

The deeper knowledge of the course of Nature in the development of ability to speak the mother tongue is thus the basis and the source of all truly mnemonic and psychological advantages with which the Art facilitates the learning by natural methods of every new language.

I turn again to the consideration of this great fundamental principle of every natural method of learning a language.

In the learning of the mother tongue Nature subjects us up to a certain point to certain fixed laws on which every natural method of language instruction is based and must be based. The mother is by her nature instinctively inclined to give this instruction and the child to receive it. The mother does not give this instruction instinctively but she is instinctively inclined toward it. The free and joyous pursuit of it is her happiness. The impulse to act in accordance with these laws is deeply implanted in the nature both of the mother and the child.

But this nature has been generally enfeebled in mothers by the artificial tendencies of our time. Placing her in an unnatural relationship toward her child they have rendered ineffective in them the operation of the laws relating to the development of the powers of speech. . . . This undermining of the influence of instinct both in the giving and in the receiving of the mother's earliest instruction is very important in its consequences. . . . Moreover the learning of every foreign language has been deprived of its naturalness through confusion that has crept into the earliest instruction of the child by the mother.

The great advantages of the natural method in the learning of the mother tongue are illustrated further in that,

from the very first, it exercises the child in all the fundamental parts of speech and by a thousand repetitions makes
the child's knowledge of these clear, and his use of them,
ready. This is so true, that, in this way, not only the essential nature of every individual part of speech is brought,
indefinitely, but firmly, before the consciousness of the
elementary pupil, but also the inflections of every substan-
tive, adjective and pronoun, that is, the inflections of every
declinable part of speech are practised and made habitual.
The uninflected parts of speech, the adverbs, prepositions,
conjunctions and interjections . . . can, through psychologically arranged series of examples of the part they play
in building up speech, be impressed upon the mind, and
skill in their use can be facilitated to an extent which the
course of nature, left to itself, could not attain. . . .

In this way every child who has been instructed in
language by the natural method acquires a vocabulary
capable of expressing all the knowledge he has acquired
through his perceptive faculties. He thus acquires the ability
to express himself readily and definitely without ever having found it necessary to master rules or principles of
language and without ever having had to learn, to this end,
a single word by heart.

Nevertheless the principle that the methods of learning a
foreign language are identical with those by which the
mother tongue is learned, is one from which the refined
artificiality of our time (which has been especially influential in introducing confusion and difficulty into elementary
instruction in foreign languages) has diverted public attention. It is firmly grounded, however, in the sound
common sense of human nature. It is a fact that the less a

person who wishes to train a child in the use of a foreign language knows about the routine of conventional language instruction the more likely he is to employ principles and methods which are in harmony with the course of nature in the development of the child's mastery of her mother tongue.

Experience demonstrates beyond all controversy that the more those who are unsophisticated devote themselves to teaching a child a foreign language the more strikingly successful are their efforts. A French servant girl, who has been charged with the duty of teaching a German child French, will, if she can speak her language grammatically, bring the child, without the use of any artificial means, through mere persistent, diligent speaking, in a strikingly short time, to express himself with ease and correctness on every subject about which she has conversed with him. The routine procedure of our time through the use of the ordinary conventional methods can accomplish this neither in private instruction nor in our public schools. If one asks now, what gives this uneducated girl the advantage over the regular teachers of a foreign language . . . it is evident that it is the similarity of her procedure to that of the course of nature in leading the young to the mastery of every mother tongue in the world. The child, who is to acquire from her some knowledge of the French language, hears for a long time a great many French words of whose meaning he has no idea; at the same time it is the presence of the objects to his senses which gives him the connection of the French words with the language itself and with visual sense impressions and leads him to recognize the word as the expression of these. Thus in the instruction given by this servant girl the knowledge of the names of qualities, and activities is added to that of the names of the objects, the principal words, just as in the learning of the mother tongue: and the entire list of words which he has learned from the girl, is drilled into his memory by manifold repetitions and phrase combinations. Just as in the mother tongue, the phraseology brings all the essential parts of speech bound together in a unity to consciousness at once, and intensifies the impression of all through innumerable repetitions, different and peculiar in each case. The words of the language to be learned and their inflections are thus mastered, as regards their meaning and pronunciation, without the learner knowing how and without the trouble of learning by heart or of the fatiguing expositions which are customary in the routine methods of learning a foreign language. . . . A man who finds himself by accident in a locality where no one speaks his language and where, in consequence, he understands no one and no one understands him, must learn the new language in just the way that the French maid taught French to the German child. . . .

I proceed now to consider the object of elementary education without any further special reference to the attempt to set up a standard procedure for the learning of all languages.

Just as it is true, as regards the faculty of speech, that it is life that educates and that all of the means which really assist nature in her influence upon developing life are derived from the natural means of training the powers of observation, and, just as the means of developing the language faculty must be in harmony with the means of developing the powers of observation, so also must the means of developing the powers of thought. The connection between the powers of observation and of thought is as follows: The perceptive faculty, if it is not unnaturally confused and misled, leads man to clear ideas, regarding the objects in his environment, that is, to the fundamental materials for the natural stimulation of his thinking powers. But so far as these clear ideas are based only on sense perception they do not meet the demands of human nature. This strives to raise these sense impressions, to clear ideas; it strives by the exercise of its own power to combine, to separate and to compare the objects of sense perception; it strives to use these as a means of training its powers of judgment. It desires to work them over logically. It must desire it. Its innate capacity for thought and judgment compels it. Everyone uses this power; everyone thinks and judges. And the art of facilitating the transition from clear consciousness of objects of perception to correct thought and judgment regarding them through naturally organized and psychologically ordered means, lies within our power. For untold ages men have sought to facilitate this transition and to raise common sense to the status of logically certified processes of thought and judgment. But the routine methods of training the powers of observation and language have abandoned the path of nature. . . . The same thing is true also as regards those methods which the destructive artificiality of our time has made almost universal in the training of our powers of thought.

Unquestionably the natural course of the art of training the capacity for thought must be brought into harmony with the thought-training which life affords, and just as man acquires the power of love and faith not through explanatory descriptions but through the actual experience of love and faith so he can attain mastery in the field of thought, not through an explanation of the laws of human thought, but through actual thinking. The elementary system of training which is adapted to promote the natural development of the powers of thought recognizes in number the simplest means of promoting the transition from the trained powers of perception to the trained capacity for thought, and of developing and training the peculiar basis of this higher capacity, namely, the power of abstraction.

In order, however, to judge rightly of what is recognized by the Elementary Method as the foundation of the development of the powers of thought one must recognize clearly that the art of natural instruction in number and form is not a mere mechanical drill in enumerating and measuring. Nor is it merely the art of making calculations and measurements shorter and easier. . . . It consists in the simplest stimulation from within of the capacity to combine, to separate or compare independently, within ourselves, the objects of perception.

The training value of elementary instruction in form and number arises from the tendency toward activity on the part of man's thinking powers. Man must use the objects of perception as a means of learning to think about them, to combine them, to separate them and to compare them. And, while he does this, as he must do it, there develops within him the power which actuates this impulse to activity, the ability to measure and count.

The elementary science of number and form is a product of man's original, innate powers of thought and of his ability to combine, separate and compare . . . the methods of a science of number and form so conceived must harmonize in the highest degree, with the general course of nature in the development of our powers. . . . It can be shown that where this elementary training proceeds in the path marked out by nature, its methods are adapted to lead pupils, quickly and surely, step by step, from the elements of number and form to the independent solution of by no means easy problems in algebra and geometry.

By this it is by no means meant that elementary pupils of all classes are to be trained to an extensive knowledge of algebra and geometry. The different classes and social ranks, and even the different individuals in these, do not require the same degree of instruction. Only a very few of them need a notably high degree of training; and it is actually desirable that, among the children of all ranks, only those should receive advanced training, who, in the lower classes, have made such remarkable progress and have developed such a high degree of interest and enthusiasm as to show that they are endowed with unusual abilities for this work.

But when such extraordinary powers do manifest themselves, society should recognize its special obligation to develop them.

DEVELOPMENT OF PRACTICAL SKILL

I pass now to a presentation of my views as to the elementary development of practical skill.

Practical skill, previous to its development, is, like every other faculty of mankind, only talent, or capacity. This, like the capacity for observation, speech or thought, develops only through exercise, through use, to practical skill. Its training begins, of course, with that of the sense organs and the limbs. The inner spiritual nature of all practical skill is intimately related to that of intellectual training and of the faculty of thought. All elementary means of the natural development of the thinking powers are essentially, also, natural means of the development of the inner nature of all practical skill. Just as number and form are naturally well adapted to strengthen and improve our powers of logical thought through affording, and progressively developing, exercises in combining, separating and comparing objects of perception, just so they are adapted to develop and strengthen the intellectual side of practical skill in common with the powers of thought and judgment. The external and internal factors of practical skill, however, must be developed together from the cradle up and must be brought into action in the most intimate connection with each other, and put into use in such a way as to afford training. . . . The inner essence of practical skill like that of the faculties of perception, speech and thought is intellect and life. The external means of the development of practical skill are physical in so far as they require the development of the senses and sense organs, and in so far as they require the training of our limbs they are mechanical. Both require an elementary gymnastic of the senses, the sense organs and the limbs. The principles and methods of the gymnastic of the senses and of the sense organs must be abstracted from the physical laws innate in these faculties which the gymnastic must strengthen and develop. . . .

The innate impulse to activity of each of the child's

faculties leads him to employ the many-sided capacities of his senses and limbs.

He proceeds independently, in advance of the assisting art. The supplementary training must not precede the free activity of the untrained impulse to practical activity. Its influence should be merely stimulating. It must arouse the feeling "I can do that," stimulate the child to the imitation of a beautiful sound. It must place chalk, a lead pencil, or a piece of charcoal in the child's hand, and, without interfering or wishing to correct, allow him to make straight and crooked lines in the form of crosses, or otherwise. When the child voluntarily imitates the easy words and pleasant sounds and begins to take pleasure in changing his drawings and making them more accurate, when the thought occurs to him, "My dear Mother can help me in making what I want to make," that is the time for deliberate, systematic instruction. . . .

The means of training to skill in any art arise partly from the sensory needs of our physical nature, partly from intellectual impulses and tendencies and partly from the nature of the art itself. The most advanced stages in the art of architecture had their beginnings in the efforts of the savage to beautify his reed hut. Had our race never had any need of shelter against wind and weather, man would never have had any palaces. If we had never had the desire to cross from one shore of a river or lake to another we should probably have had few of our many kinds of ships. . . .

Only when we have to a marked degree satisfied these needs of our primitive nature does the art impulse naturally lead us farther and endeavor to employ the artistic powers which have been tested and strengthened in the satisfaction of our primitive needs, for the gratification of our intellectual impulses and inclinations. It extends its beneficent influence on the training of the human race in general, only in so far as it remains in harmony with the source out of which it has sprung. . . .

The lack of genuineness and accuracy in the work of the common, bread-winning, domestic and civic classes, illustrates this. . . .

The principle, "It is life that educates," is less generally applicable in the higher ranks of society than in the lower, if one has in mind the wholesome, natural influence of home life on the education of humanity both as regards the naturalness of its means and the beneficence of its results. The lower classes will be trained in many ways from the cradle up in the essentials of the mechanical skill which they will need throughout their lives. The children of the peasants, of the manual laborer, and of all classes who maintain their households through their earnings, live from morning to night amidst surroundings and relationships in which they continually find occasion and incitement to acquire skill in the occupation of the father, and to acquire the essentials of any special skill required for a vocation suited to their condition and circumstances. With the upper classes this is not at all the case. They derive no aid from want and necessity. With a self-complacency born of their circumstances their children say: "I am rich and have been rich and I have no need of it." That benevolent feeling of the children of the common people of the city and the country: "I can help my dear father and mother in their work, even in that which they can carry on only in the sweat of the brow." This benevolent feeling of the children of the common classes, and the domestic preparation for adequate training in the mechanical skill of some occupation suited to their circumstances, is lacking to the children of the upper classes and still more to the children of the countless swarm of pretenders who in their idleness and worthlessness wish to be considered, not as of the common people, where they really belong, but as hangers-on of the wealthy and aristocratic people who live in their vicinity. . . .

The superficiality of our routine procedure leads usually to thoughtless chatter about the objects through which we should instruct ourselves. If a child does not understand what he should learn, and yet has to show that he does understand it, he is led to engage in thoughtless talk about subjects which he does not understand. . . .

True as this is, it is no less true that the means of warding off the harmful influence of artifice, and of paving the way to the true art of education are to be found in the Elementary Method. Its force is derived from the influence which the simplification of the means of education and instruction in its entirety has, and must have, on the culture of the human race; and it is through this simplification that it is enabled to exalt the educational influence of home life and of its centre, the living-room, and thereby to set in motion for education a million forces which at present lie dormant and unutilized.

As a corollary of this truth I shall add only this: Every child, as we already know, in consequence of the simplification of his instructional material, is in a position to impart to his brothers and sisters, and to any other child, what he has learned at each stage of development; and to every well-conducted child it is a joy to do this, just as it would be a pleasure to every unsophisticated mother to aid him in this as far as possible. It is an indisputable fact that children infinitely prefer to be shown how to do something by other children rather than by any adult who does not possess either a strikingly delicate and motherly disposition or an equally powerful fatherly heart.

But it is an undeniable truth that the Elementary Method develops this capacity in every child who has been well trained in accordance with its principles. The importance of this lies in the fact that it proves conclusively that all genuine and thoroughly prosecuted means of education are adapted to make the children capable of assisting their parents just as much morally and intellectually in the general education of their brothers and sisters as poverty and necessity incite them, in every household which depends for its daily bread upon manual labor, to assist materially and economically.

So certain is it that even the recognition of the Elementary Method would set in motion a million dormant educational influences and that, in general, the beneficent effect upon domestic life, if it were actually adopted, would be incalculable. Its principles and methods constitute nothing less than a new doctrine. The world has always recognized the essential truths on which it is based, although these have never been verbally expressed in accordance with our views. In my youth in ordinary households I have heard a hundred times the statement: "A child who from early youth on has learned to pray, think and work is already half educated." . . . This clearly shows that the Elementary

Method in its entirety is nothing other than a carefully and exhaustively constructed psychological supplement to the course of nature in the development of our moral, intellectual, and physical powers. . . .

The consequences which psychologically well-organized efforts to strengthen the educational influences of the home life through a simplification of the means employed must have on the human race are to be traced in the early life of the child in the all-round development of his powers, and are an outgrowth of this. . . .

The Elementary Method is not restricted in its influence to the development of man's powers of thought. It embraces the whole circle of our scientific, art, and professional knowledge and skill. . . .

Just as no child lives without a certain amount of direct knowledge of objects of his environment which has become mature, so every child whose powers of speech have been trained according to the Elementary Method, that is, to the same extent as his powers of observation, has reached a point at which his knowledge, derived from observation, borders upon scientific knowledge.

Let us take an example from natural history. Every child even though it lives in the most straitened circumstances knows at least six mammals, and an equal number of fish, birds, insects, amphibians and worms. If the child observes these few animals accurately from the cradle on, in accordance with the Elementary Method, knows them correctly in all their essential parts and different qualities, and can express himself definitely in regard to these . . . such a child has made a beginning toward acquiring a scientific knowledge of mammals, of ornithology, of ichthyology, etc. And if circumstances permit or require him to master these sciences his previous training has thoroughly prepared him for the task.

Further, it is no less true that if the child has been naturally trained in observation and in number and form it has been no less thoroughly prepared for scientific work through the knowledge of reckoning, drawing and measuring which it has acquired.

In all sciences the same holds true. The natural powers of observation, of speech; the knowledge and mastery of number and form that have been acquired through the Elementary Method have in all branches of knowledge the same effect; whether it be pure or applied sciences, whether it be professional knowledge or skill, or knowledge of any kind whatsoever the Elementary Methods of training the human powers has the same effect. I say it with conviction; the Elementary Method is equal to all this or it is nothing at all. Its value, its great value, lies partly in ourselves and partly in our surroundings and educational impressions from which are not lacking to any man. Every child, for instance, who has learned to observe accurately the changes in water at rest or in motion which take place every day before our eyes, its various forms of dew, rain, moisture, fog, frost, hail, etc., and the effect of these on the condition of other natural objects, and has learned to express himself with accuracy about them, has already taken the first steps toward an artistic appreciation or a scientific treatment of them. Again every child who has observed, with "elementary" accuracy, the solution of salt and of sugar in the kitchen and the reverse change from a liquid to a solid, crystalline state, and, similarly, the fermentation of wine and its change to vinegar in the cellar, the change of alabaster into gypsum, or marble into lime, or sand into glass and has learned to express himself with accuracy in regard to these, has made a beginning in that objective knowledge of the sciences whose further, more detailed investigation these objects require. In the same way a child who has observed with "Elementary" accuracy a few peasants' houses in all their parts and has learned to express himself with accuracy regarding them, may, if he possesses exceptional talent, and if his observations have been supported by "Elementary" exercises in number and form, enter upon a career as an architect. . . .

Adhering firmly to the lofty principle, "It is life that educates," and, in its extension, growing out of the natural educational procedure of domestic life, the Elementary Method, because of its nature, avoids the paths of confusion and error into which the superficial methods characteristic of our people and our time are leading millions of individuals to their destruction. The means of true elementary education are, in the entire scope of their application, mind and life, just as they are these in their origin and development. This is so far true, that even as regards the false routine instruction in the sciences, which has no foundation in actually observed facts and from which young children derive little educational benefit; it may nevertheless be said, that the principles of the Elementary Method are adapted to show how even such sciences may be learned in as natural a manner as possible, and to direct to means for accomplishing this end.

In support of this view I cite geography and history. I am, of course, far from recognizing these as suitable subjects for elementary instruction. But if one, rightly or wrongly, wishes to have one of these subjects taught, the principles of the Elementary Method will lead in geography simply and naturally to the easiest method of drill on the names of mountains, rivers, cities and other localities and to an easy, objective method of fixing in the mind the relative location of these. These double exercises are in the highest degree adapted to the nature of the child. His memory and his powers of observation are in full vigor and, to a high degree, receptive to all that affects the senses. Hence I should train a child, who wishes to learn geography, not only in the observation of the positions and relationships of the places in his immediate vicinity but I should drill him in his earliest language and reading lessons in the names of the cities and towns of a given region, e. g., a river basin, in the order and sequence in which they occur on the map until he could pronounce them in proper succession with sufficient readiness.

And just as in learning to speak it is a helpful preparation for the later knowledge of the objects, whose name the child is learning to pronounce, if the names can be impressed upon his ear and readily pronounced long before the objects themselves are thoroughly known; so also a knowledge of the names of places in their sequence on the map is excellent preparation for later geographical studies. . . . This method of learning geography has for children of this age a marked influence in strengthening the memory for names and places.

The same is true of the drill in history tried out with young children. Unless one wishes to destroy in children all sense of the nature and inner spirit of history and to make them incapable of studying it, one should not attempt to teach it as such even when the child is taking his first steps in science. It is utter nonsense to attempt to acquaint men with the spirit of past ages, when they are not yet acquainted with the present world which lies before them. Hence with such children one can go no farther in the study of history than to drill them well in an extended historical nomenclature and in familiarizing them with localities, a knowledge of which history requires. I look upon these exercises with the skeleton outlines of history and geography as nothing other than a sort of mnemonic language drill. . . .

However, I conclude this subject and proceed from a limited and one-sided view of the "Elementary" means of cultivating the powers of observation, language, thought and practical skill to a general comprehensive view of the inner nature of the Elementary Method.

I must do so; for if it has been demonstrated beyond dispute that the "Elementary" methods of cultivating the intellectual and practical capacities of the child, well carried out, will, by their simplicity, train the child, stimulate him and bring him to make very satisfactory and very striking progress in observation, language, thought and practical skill, respectively, this is not saying that through progress in each of these powers, individually, the essential needs of humanity have been naturally and adequately met.

The true, natural *common* power of human nature is a product, as we know, of an effort to harmonize all *individual* human powers among themselves and working upon these intellectual and practical powers individually does not accomplish this at all. It leads on the contrary to an effort on the part of each to dominate over the others. It becomes in this way, plainly, the definite, original source of a war of all against all.

Hence it becomes clear that the question, "What is natural in education and instruction?" can be rightly answered and the idea of naturalness can be correctly conceived only when the question "What is human nature itself?" has been cleared up. This consists, however, in the essence of humanity itself, in those inner divine powers which we share with no other creature on earth.

Even the ox has mind and life; not the mind of man, however, but only that of the beast. . . . The mind of our race (in so far as it is merely instinctive and sensory) reveals itself neither in thought nor in faith as a distinctively human mind: these are both powers which we possess in common with the beasts of the field. As regards the senses, through which the lower animals as well as ourselves acquire a knowledge of the world, they are often better equipped than we. The dog has a more efficient nose; the eagle a better eye than man. And this holds true of the various uses to which animals apply their powers. These seem to us in many instances to border upon the marvelous and as representing a degree of skill unattainable by man. But their art is not human art. It is only the result of an instinctive power, whose nature, indeed, the greatest human intellect is unable to fathom, but whose difference from human art and from the human power of thought on which this is based is evident to everyone. . . .

The vastness of the difference between the lowest in human and the highest in merely animal nature is so striking that in my mind the saying of David, "Thou hast

274

made us a little lower than the angels," associates itself with the saying, "Thou hast raised us infinitely above all flesh and blood that wanders upon the earth, thou hast made us superior to the beasts of the field."

In order not to leave the meaning of "naturalness" uncertain and indefinite we must bear in mind that the "Elementary" intellectual and practical training of our race is fitted to produce a general human power which combines all the beneficent influences of all our individual capacities; this general power arises from a harmony of our faculties which affects our acts of commission and omission and those fundamental powers of human nature on which our feeling, thinking and action are based.

Where one of these powers is weak, crippled and untrained, or, still more, mistrained, the common power of human nature lacks the basis requisite to the exercise by the other two of an adequately beneficent influence.

We must not overlook the fact that, in the strictest sense of the word, absolute harmony of the human faculties is unthinkable. . . . All that has been said in regard to a harmony of the human powers is to be understood as referring to a state which approximates to harmony. . . .

The truth that the degree of harmony of which our race is capable is attainable to a like degree under all conditions of human life is connected with the truth that it is attainable only when love and faith are present. And here it must not be forgotten that true faith and true love without a general love of truth is unthinkable. . . .

They are certainly wrong who abandon themselves to the delusion that what is so urgently needed will be supplied without our cooperation. Neither the talent for love nor faith nor those for thought, and practical skill are cultivated in individuals, much less in our different social classes without our assistance.

Just as this lofty idea of Elementary Method requires careful attention to the psychological foundation of the sequence of the means of education and harmony among these, it demands also that these should be in harmony with conditions and circumstances peculiar to the different social ranks, respectively. Attention to this ensures that the child in all social ranks, learns to love what is worthy of love in his peculiar station, to think about that in his surroundings which appeals to thought and that he learns from the cradle up, to act, wish, hope and strive for that which, in his condition in life, seems desirable, necessary and useful. . . . If it is the child of a peasant the Elementary Methods of training will make of him, neither as regards his feelings, his intellect nor his practical skill, a dreamy impractical creature, an outcast from the peasant class, incapable of rightly estimating the worth of his class or of contributing to its improvement. . . .

The rehabilitation of the different classes requires different measures. The urban classes do not need a more thorough general training than the peasant but they need a notably different kind of training. If the adequately trained peasant must be trained so that he will not have to call in the cabinet-maker whenever a board has to be planed, nor the blacksmith and locksmith whenever a nail is to be driven into the wall, so the city artisan class must be trained to appreciate the different objects of art needed in the different vocations with mathematical accuracy and esthetic taste, to solve number problems algebraically and to handle problems of form with trained inventiveness and mathematical correctness.

The welfare of the urban middle class depends upon the extent to which they as a class are trained to participate personally in the various trades and occupations. . . .

Necessity compels the lower classes to acquire this practical skill.

This is not the case with the aristocracy. They neither can nor should be led through manual to intellectual activity nor through these to the elevation of their emotional nature. They must be guided and stimulated through the cultivation of the heart and of the intellect to the employment of the hand. . . .

The prosperity of the productive classes, urban as well as rural, depends upon the cultivation of their ability to do. The extension of knowledge contributes very little. The upper classes, on the other hand, need as a distinguishing characteristic of their system of education, a considerable extension of knowledge, but of knowledge based upon personal observation. The practical capacity which they need depends upon the extent and the thoroughness of their knowledge. . . . Those who are to be trained for the learned class should have an education distinguished by a more thoroughly intellectual and investigative enquiry into the real inner nature of the objects, the scientific investigation and intellectual treatment of which, is their vocation.

The question arises "What does Nature contribute toward the attainment of the educational ends peculiar to the different social classes, respectively?"

The reply is that the best means of training are to be found in the immediate environment of the individuals of these different classes, respectively, and especially in those objects which normally occasion activity.

The human art of education simply supplements the course of nature in the development of our powers, and is subordinate to, and in harmony with, the latter. To accomplish this a profound knowledge and a keen sensitiveness to the course of nature is required. In each case the Art can accomplish this only in so far as its means have been derived from the eternal unchanging laws of human nature and have not been destroyed by the artificial tendencies of our time. . . .

For the manual laborer the adequate development of his senses and his limbs to meet his needs constitutes the basis for the development of his powers of thought. . . . His learning to read and to write must be based upon his powers of speech.

The education of our time, both in its influence and in the means it employs is much more a result of the collective demands of our race . . . than a result of regard for the general needs of human nature itself as these find expression in every single individual. . . . It is more concerned with what is foreign to us, than it is educative for what we ourselves are and for what we as independent beings need.

The consequences of this are of the highest importance. Certainly the unrest of our time and all its bloody and windy phenomena have their origin in the ever-growing weakness of our individual powers for self-help which is every day intensified by the artificial tendencies of the present.

INDEX

INDEX

INDEX